ARE YOU A C... THE TV TR... HOUR OR F... "TRIVIA POINTS" QUESTION?

Try a little warm-up session and see.

1. What was Jack Paar's opening theme song on the *Tonight* show?
2. Name the rocket on *Rocky Jones, Space Ranger*.
3. Who played Lassie's first TV master?
4. On *Hogan's Heroes*, to what did "Papa Bear" and "Goldilocks" refer?
5. Who was Burns and Allen's postman?
6. At various times, Ethel Mertz was given three different middle names. What were they?

The answers are upside down below, and if you got them all you can hold your own in any trivia match. Even if you missed a few, you're sure to find plenty of familiar shows and stars awaiting you in **THE OFFICIAL TV TRIVIA QUIZ BOOK #3.**

BART ANDREWS is a TV comedy writer, playwright (co-author of the musical *Ape Over Broadway*), magazine journalist, and author of the book about *I Love Lucy*— *LUCY AND RICKY AND FRED AND ETHEL*.

1. "Everything's Coming Up Roses"
2. *Orbit Jet*
3. Tommy Rettig
4. They were code words for London and the Stalag 13 captives respectively.
5. Mr. Beasley
6. Louise, Mae, and Roberta

Other SIGNET Books for the Trivia Buff

- [ ] **THE OFFICIAL TV TRIVIA QUIZ BOOK** by Bart Andrews. (#Y6363—$1.25)
- [ ] **THE OFFICIAL TV TRIVIA QUIZ BOOK #2** by Bart Andrews. (#W8410—$1.50)
- [ ] **THE FABULOUS FIFTIES QUIZ BOOK** by Bart Andrews. (#W8116—$1.50)
- [ ] **FROM THE BLOB TO STAR WARS: The Science Fiction Movie Quiz Book** by Bart Andrews. (#W7948—$1.50)
- [ ] **THE TREKKIE QUIZ BOOK** by Bart Andrews. (#W8413—$1.50)
- [ ] **THE UFO MOVIE QUIZ BOOK** by Jeff Rovin. (#E8258—$1.75)*
- [ ] **THE OFFICIAL MOVIE TRIVIA QUIZ BOOK #2** by Martin A. Gross. (#W7898—$1.50)
- [ ] **THE NOSTALGIA QUIZ BOOK** by Martin A. Gross. (#W7384—$1.50)
- [ ] **THE NOSTALGIA QUIZ BOOK #2** by Martin A. Gross. (#Y6554—$1.25)
- [ ] **THE NOSTALGIA QUIZ BOOK #3** by Martin A. Gross. (#W8412—$1.50)
- [ ] **THE OFFICIAL ROCK 'N' ROLL TRIVIA QUIZ BOOK** by Marc Sotkin. (#W8485—$1.50)
- [ ] **THE OFFICIAL ROCK 'N' ROLL TRIVIA QUIZ BOOK #2** by Marc Sotkin. (#E8299—$1.75)*
- [ ] **THE BEATLES TRIVIA QUIZ BOOK** by Helen Rosenbaum. (#W8225—$1.50)
- [ ] **THE ELVIS PRESLEY TRIVIA QUIZ BOOK** by Helen Rosenbaum. (#W8178—$1.50)

* Price slightly higher in Canada

THE NEW AMERICAN LIBRARY, INC.,
P.O. Box 999, Bergenfield, New Jersey 07621

Please send me the SIGNET BOOKS I have checked above. I am enclosing $_____(please add 50¢ to this order to cover postage and handling). Send check or money order—no cash or C.O.D.'s. Prices and numbers are subject to change without notice.

Name_____

Address_____

City_____State_____Zip Code_____

Allow at least 4 weeks for delivery

THE OFFICIAL TV TRIVIA QUIZ BOOK #3

1,001 Nostalgia Questions for Television Addicts

---

by Bart Andrews

A SIGNET BOOK
NEW AMERICAN LIBRARY
TIMES MIRROR

To Robert Earle Haynie,
who started me on this
road to ruinous rewards.
Thank you, Bob.

NAL BOOKS ARE ALSO AVAILABLE AT DISCOUNTS IN BULK QUANTITY FOR INDUSTRIAL OR SALES-PROMOTIONAL USE. FOR DETAILS, WRITE TO PREMIUM MARKETING DIVISION, NEW AMERICAN LIBRARY, INC., 1301 AVENUE OF THE AMERICAS, NEW YORK, NEW YORK 10019.

COPYRIGHT © 1978 BY BART ANDREWS

All rights reserved

The photos in this book are from the collection of Howard Frank. Copies of these and other nostalgia pictures are available by writing Personality Photos, Inc., Box 50, Brooklyn, New York 11230.

SIGNET TRADEMARK REG. U.S. PAT. OFF. AND FOREIGN COUNTRIES
REGISTERED TRADEMARK—MARCA REGISTRADA
HECHO EN CHICAGO, U.S.A.

SIGNET, SIGNET CLASSICS, MENTOR, PLUME AND MERIDIAN BOOKS
are published by The New American Library, Inc.,
1301 Avenue of the Americas, New York, New York 10019

FIRST PRINTING, NOVEMBER, 1978

1 2 3 4 5 6 7 8 9

PRINTED IN THE UNITED STATES OF AMERICA

Channel One

There is nothing wrong with your television set. Do not attempt to adjust the picture. I am controlling transmission. For the next few hours, sit quietly and I will control all that you see. You are about to participate in a great adventure; you are about to experience the awe and mystery which reaches from the inner mind to the outer limits of TV trivia.

As a TV buff, you *should* know where I lifted that opening. If not, have no fear—there are 1,001 other questions for you.

First, I should thank you for buying this book. (If you're browsing in a bookstore right now and have no intention of adding this wonderful paperback to your library, may your TV forever roll.) It warms my heart to know that there are "trivial" people out there in TV-land, folks who are serious in their search for minutiae and esoterica about our beloved boob tube.

In fact, some of you have helped prepare this labor of love—*you* know who you are! I thank Gerald Osher, Robert J. West, Dan Coviello, Jeffrey Judson, Jr. (America's foremost *Howdy Doody* collector), Robert Meister, Stephen L. Eberly, Steve Petersen, Bill Dunning, Harry Czaplinski (and the other members of Zoo), David Burd, Patricia Ann Anders, Greg Maiuro, Mindy Levine, Philip Robins, David Stanley, David P. Strauss (author of *Hollywood Trivia*), Garnett Harris, Jr., and Chuck Fulton for your interesting contributions.

By the way, you, too, can be a part of TV Trivia by sending along your questions and answers (make sure they're correct—I hate being called an idiot) to me at Box 727, Hollywood, California 90028, and get *your* name in the next book.

Also, thanks to a few friends—Mike Spindell of radio station WNWS in Miami, Jim Eason of San Francisco's KGO, Sally Jesse Raphael at WMCA in New York City, WRNG's answer to Scarlett O'Hara—Atlanta's own Ludlow Porch, Jim Christian of WERC in Birmingham, and Robert L. Smith of *Channel One* magazine for helping to keep TV Trivia alive and well.

My assistant Brad Dunning deserves a nod, too—he helped to put this book together—and so does Maureen McCaffrey at the Nostalgia Book Club for "spreading the word."

In closing, I hope you enjoy this new collection of trivial queries. It was a *real* treat assembling it for you.

BART ANDREWS

Hollywood, California

QUESTIONS

1. "I LOVE LUCY"

1. Where did Lucy Ricardo stomp grapes?
2. Who was the head of the Ricardo clan in Cuba?
3. For whom was the loving cup that Lucy got stuck on her head intended?
4. Who gave Lucy and Ethel the giant walk-in meat freezer?
5. What song could Lucy play on the saxophone?
6. Who played Ricky's Tropicana nightclub boss Alvin Littlefield?
7. How did Lucy attempt to smuggle a twenty-five-pound hunk of Italian cheese into the United States?
8. What make of vacuum cleaner did Lucy once buy?
9. Who were the Ricardos' next-door neighbors in Connecticut?
10. Who originally sponsored the show?

2. COMMERCIAL QUIZ

Match the program or star with the appropriate 1955 sponsor.

1. *Father Knows Best*
2. *The Lawrence Welk Show*
3. *Sergeant Preston of the Yukon*
4. *The People's Choice*
5. Patti Page
6. *Make Room for Daddy*
7. *Ramar of the Jungle*
8. *Racket Squad*
9. *The Phil Silvers Show*
10. *Captain Gallant of the Foreign Legion*
11. *Professional Father*

a. Helene Curtis
b. Oldsmobile
c. Scott Paper Company
d. Camel
e. Quaker Puffed Wheat
f. Good 'n' Plenty
g. Dodge
h. Bordens
i. Heinz
j. Philip Morris
k. Pall Mall

3. MEDIA MAGIC

1. The characters were Ben Calhoun, Dave Tarrant, Barnabus Rogers, and Nils. Name the series.

2. What did Stanley Andrews, Ronald Reagan, Robert Taylor, and Dale Robertson have in common?

3. Name Britt Reid's automobile.

4. Who was the leader of The Secret Squadron?

5. What was Wild Bill Hickok's full name?

6. With what western hero would you associate Russ Hayden?

7. What role did Ed Wynn play on the *Playhouse 90* presentation of *Requiem for a Heavyweight*?

8. Complete this message: "Hi, I'm Buster Brown; I live in a shoe. That's my dog _____; he lives in there, too."

9. Who hosted *The Stork Club*?

10. Who owned the Straightaway Garage?

11. In what New England town was *Willy* set?

4. BIGAMY

Name the actor who played husband to both actresses, and name the programs.

1. Mary Tyler Moore and Hope Lange
2. Aneta Corseaut and Lee Meriweather
3. Betty White and Evelyn Scott
4. Joan Davis and Natalie Schafer
5. Jody Warner and Elizabeth Montgomery
6. Lurene Tuttle and Ruth Warrick
7. Bea Benaderet and Edna Skinner
8. Ann McCrea and Trisha Hart
9. Emmaline Henry and Carolyn Jones
10. Rosemary DeCamp and Audrey Meadows

5. BACK IN THE SADDLE

1. Which western constituted the actual retelling of the story of Billy the Kid and Pat Garrett?
2. Who played Jesse James on TV?
3. What was the setting of *Lawman*?
4. What kind of rifle did Lucas McCain carry?
5. What was Doc Adams's first name on *Gunsmoke*?
6. Name the TV western that was transformed into a radio show in 1958.
7. What was the name of Wild Bill Hickok's steed?
8. Why did the Lone Ranger use silver bullets?
9. Who portrayed Kit Carson on television?
10. What now-famous movie stars once played ranch hands on *Empire*?
11. What was the Lone Ranger's real name?

6. THE FIRST TIME

Match the following performers with the programs on which they made their television debuts.

1. Garry Moore   a. *Toast of the Town*
2. Marilyn Monroe   b. *You Bet Your Life*
3. Audrey Meadows   c. *The Ed Wynn Show*
4. Phyllis Diller   d. *The Adventures of Ozzie and Harriet*
5. Elvis Presley   e. *Stage Show*
6. The Beatles   f. *Ford Star Jubilee*
7. Mary Tyler Moore   g. *The Ed Sullivan Show*
8. Carol Burnett   h. *Pantomime Quiz*
9. Judy Garland   i. *The Jack Benny Show*
10. Lucille Ball   j. *The Paul Winchell-Jerry Mahoney Show*

7. SPINOFFS

From what popular series were these shows created?

1. *Maude*
2. *Gomer Pyle, U.S.M.C.*
3. *The Andy Griffith Show*
4. *Rhoda*
5. *Fish*
6. *Dirty Sally*
7. *Happy Days*
8. *Pete and Gladys*
9. *Green Acres*
10. *Adventures of Champion*

8. TELE-VERSIONS

1. On *The Andy Griffith Show*, Warren Ferguson was whose nephew?
2. *The Fugitive* was wanted for murder in what state?
3. What chess piece adorned Paladin's calling cards?
4. Where did Fonzie work before opening his own garage?
5. Who killed Mrs. Helen Kimble?
6. Name Eddie Munster's wolfman doll.
7. Before the war, what type of factory did Sergeant Hans Schultz own?
8. What is the name of Jacques Cousteau's ship?
9. From what station house did the *Emergency* squad operate?
10. Who is Alice's faithful boyfriend on *The Brady Bunch*?

9. "THE WILD, WILD WEST"

1. What were Artemus Gordon and Jim West's previous professions?
2. Name at least two other men who were, at one time, Jim West's partners.
3. Who were Durk DeJohn, Pierre Gasper, Uncle Moe, Colonel Cross, Lightnin' McCoy, and Fedore Rimsky?
4. Who were Colonels Richmond and Crockett?
5. Name the President whom Jim and Artie were assigned to protect.
6. Who were Anabella, Arabella, and Henry and Henrietta?
7. Who was Tennison?
8. What was the duo's main mode of transportation?
9. Who played Dr. Miguelito Coyote Loveless?
10. What network carried the popular adventure series?

10. VIDEO VILLAINS

Match the "bad guy" with the program on which he was featured.

1. Wo Fat
2. Harry Mudd
3. Mink Fink
4. Angelique
5. Trigger Happy
6. Jordan Braddock
7. Sy Horton
8. Oscar Pudney
9. Miss Witchiepoo
10. Frank Nitti

a. *Dark Shadows*
b. *The Immortal*
c. *Hawaii Five-0*
d. *H. R. Pufnstuf*
e. *The Adventures of Superman*
f. *The Ann Sothern Show*
g. *Star Trek*
h. *Disneyland*
i. *The Untouchables*
j. *Howdy Doody*

11. OUT OF THIS WORLD

1. Commander Buzz Corey, Cadet Happy, Dr. Von Meter, and Tonga appeared in what science fiction series?

2. Who was Gene Roddenberry's original choice for the Spock role on *Star Trek?* (Hint: He later starred on another successful science fiction program.)

3. Name the rocket on *Rocky Jones, Space Ranger.*

4. Who was TV's Dr. Zarkov in the *Flash Gordon* series?

5. Who employed a "magic belt" to assume the state of invisibility?

6. Complete this series title: *Buck Rogers in the _____ Century.*

7. Who were George, Jane, Judy, and Elroy better known as?

8. The characters were Colonel Raeburn, Captain Larry Dart, Husky the Martian, and Slim the Venusian. Name the series.

9. What was the name of the rocket ship on *Lost in Space?*

10. Who was "an indestructible super-powered robot" created by widower Dr. Boynton?

12. CALL A DOCTOR

Match the doctor with the series in which he was featured.

1. Doc Williams
2. Dr. McCann
3. Dr. Edward H. Dudley
4. Dr. Judson McKay
5. Dr. Theodore Basset
6. Dr. Peter Goldstone
7. Dr. Michael Rhodes
8. Dr. Bill Baxter
9. Dr. Steve Hardy
10. Dr. Ted Steffen

a. *The Eleventh Hour*
b. *The Adventures of Ozzie and Harriet*
c. *The Doctors and the Nurses*
d. *The Sixth Sense*
e. *Frontier Doctor*
f. *Noah's Ark*
g. *Don't Call Me Charlie!*
h. *The Interns*
i. *General Hospital*
j. *The Munsters*

13. WHAT A DOG!

Name the canine character described herein.

1. Terrier on *The Thin Man*
2. German shepherd on *Longstreet*
3. Bloodhound on *The Beverly Hillbillies*
4. Great Dane on *Diana*
5. German shepherd on *The Inspector*
6. Cocker spaniel on *Marge and Jeff*
7. Great Dane on *Blansky's Beauties*
8. St. Bernard on *Topper*
9. Sheepdog on *Please Don't Eat the Daisies*
10. Sheepdog on *The Doris Day Show*

14. NIFTY FIFTIES

1. On *Amos 'n' Andy,* who were Sapphire's brother and sister?
2. Who was the strongman on *Big Top?*
3. Who played *Public Defender* Bart Matthews?
4. Who was Boris Badenov's aide?
5. Who hosted *Hollywood Today?*
6. What did James Daly, Jerome Thor, and Gerald Mohr have in common?
7. Who did an unbilled walk-on (à la Hitchcock) on each episode of *Dear Phoebe?*
8. On *The Goldbergs,* who was Uncle David's son, and what was his profession?
9. Where did George Jefferson work before going into the dry cleaning business?
10. Name Hawkeye Pierce's hometown.

15. FOREIGN PHRASES

You don't have to be a linguist to tackle this quiz. Simply identify the series from their foreign titles.

1. *Deuses de Barro*
2. *Oh Maine Nichte*
3. *Haciaelhorizonte*
4. *Adventureros del Mississippi*
5. *Estampida*
6. *Carovana*
7. *Beaver Chian*
8. *Adventuras Submarinas*
9. *Los Invencibles*
10. *Tempera de Aco*

16. VIDEO VILLAGES

Match the home addresses of the principals with the series.

1. 822 Sycamore Road, Hillsdale
2. 704 Houser Street, Queens
3. 35 Hillview Drive, Easy Valley
4. 123 Marshall Road, Hydesberg
5. 627 Elm Street, Hillsdale
6. 328 Chauncey Street, Brooklyn
7. 310 Orange Drive, Cocoa Beach
8. 730 Hansen Street, Milwaukee
9. 1164 Morning Glory Circle, Westport
10. 366 North Crandon Drive, Beverly Hills

a. *Dennis the Menace*
b. *The Adventures of Ozzie and Harriet*
c. *Bewitched*
d. *The Jack Benny Program*
e. *The Honeymooners*
f. *Hazel*
g. *All in the Family*
h. *The Jimmy Stewart Show*
i. *Laverne and Shirley*
j. *I Dream of Jeannie*

17. "LASSIE"

1. Who played Lassie's first TV master?
2. What was Jeff's mother's name?
3. Who owned Pokey?
4. What part did George Chandler portray?
5. Who played Ruth and Paul Martin, Timmy's parents?
6. What was the name of Jeff's colt?
7. Where did the Martins eventually move?
8. Who was the Millers' telephone operator?
9. What role did Robert Bray portray?
10. Who owned the Holden Ranch on which Lassie lived?

18. TV TALK

With whom would you identify these famous quotes?

1. "What sort of a day was it?"
2. "Good night and good luck."
3. "Good night and a good tomorrow."
4. "Good night, sisters."
5. "Our next millionaire, Mike."
6. "You know, you don't hardly get those no more."
7. "Ya'll come back now, ya hear."
8. "Goodnight, Mrs. Calabash."
9. "Good night and God bless."
10. "Peace."

19. CARTOON CAPERS

1. What was the policeman's name on *Top Cat?*
2. Where was Bullwinkle born?
3. What was Wilma Flintstone's maiden name?
4. "When you feel your life's in danger; when you're threatened by a stranger; when you feel that you will get a lickin' . . . " began what cartoon program?
5. Who provided the voices for The Chipmunks?
6. On *Crusader Rabbit*, what was Ragland T. "Rags" Tiger's middle name?
7. How did Bamm Bamm become a member of the Rubble family?
8. Name Johnny Quest's father.
9. Who narrated *Fractured Fairy Tales?*
10. Name the pet store that was home to Magilla Gorilla.

20. KOOKIE TALK

Kookie, the young parking lot attendant on *77 Sunset Strip,* had his own peculiar jargon. Match these Kookie-isms with their meanings.

1. Mushroom people
2. Buzzed by germsville
3. A Washington
4. Antsville
5. Like her heels were on fire
6. It's real nervous
7. Lid of your cave
8. Pile up the Z's
9. You're getting the beat
10. The long and airy

a. Door to your office
b. In a hurry
c. Put into the hospital
d. An airplane ride
e. Sleep, snore
f. You're beginning to understand
g. Those who come out at night to live it up
h. A dollar bill
i. A place full of people
j. It's good

21. WHICH ONE DOESN'T BELONG?

From each group, select one entry which should not be included, and explain why.

1. a) Harriet Nelson, b) Mary Livingston, c) Gracie Allen, d) Alice Gobel

2. a) *The Good Guys,* b) *I'm Dickens, He's Fenster,* c) *Gilligan's Island,* d) *The Many Loves of Dobie Gillis*

3. a) John McIntyre, b) Ward Bond, c) Lee J. Cobb, d) Charles Bickford

4. a) Lee Tracy, b) Mark Stevens, c) Lloyd Nolan, d) Craig Stevens

5. a) Anthony Eisley, b) Burt Reynolds, c) James MacArthur, d) Connie Stevens

6. a) *How to Marry a Millionaire,* b) *The Millionaire,* c) *The Brady Bunch,* d) *Bonanza*

7. a) *Wyatt Earp,* b) *Alfred Hitchcock Presents,* c) *Dragnet,* d) *The Big Surprise*

8. a) Wally Cox, b) Vince Edwards, c) Garry Moore, d) Raymond Burr

9. a) *The $64,000 Question,* b) *Twenty-One,* c) *Tic Tac Dough,* d) *Winky Dink and You*

10. a) Lynn Joelson, b) Audrey Peters, c) Jayne Manners, d) Pat Cotton

22. BLACK-AND-WHITES

1. Who was Phoebe B. Beebe?
2. Explain the circumstances surrounding the adoption of Joey by rancher Jim Newton on *Fury*.
3. Who hosted *See It Now*?
4. Who was Burns and Allen's postman?
5. Advice-to-the-lovelorn columnist Phoebe Goodheart was a character played by Peter Lawford in the mid-fifties. In what paper did the column appear?
6. What town was nearest to Fort Apache?
7. Who was Humphrey Higsbye?
8. Where did Mickey Mulligan work?
9. What did Pat Carroll, Peggy King, Angela Lansbury, Judith Ames, and Jeff Donnell have in common?
10. Everyone remembers Ruth Gilbert as Maxine, Milton Berle's secretary, but what character did Arnold Stang portray?

23. ALTER-EGOS

Name the actress who played wife to both actors, and name the programs.

1. David Doyle and Norman Fell
2. John Astin and Hayden Rorke
3. Bill Williams and Del Moore
4. Roy Roberts and Frank Faylen
5. Lyle Talbot and Frank Nelson
6. Leon Ames and Ransom Sherman
7. Sid Melton and Jack Kruschen
8. Bing Crosby and Fred MacMurray
9. Ernest Truex and Joseph Kearns
10. Harry Morgan and Frank Aletter

24. "CAPTAIN VIDEO"

1. Who played the first Captain Video?
2. Where was the Captain's hidden laboratory?
3. Who portrayed the youthful Video Ranger?
4. On what TV network was the show aired?
5. In what year did the adventure take place?
6. Name the Captain's spaceship.
7. What role did Dave Ballard play?
8. Captain Video was known as "The Guardian of the _____."
9. Who sponsored the series?
10. What was the purpose of the Remote Tele-Carrier?

25. PLATOON PALS

Can you identify the military series by these groups of characters?

1. Boylo, Carter, Slater, Hacker
2. Bronsky, Hale, Shafer, Blair
3. Troy, Moffitt, Pettigrew, Dietrich
4. Savage, Crowe, Stovall, Kaiser
5. Butcher, Riddle, Miller, Tyler
6. Hanley, Saunders, Kirby, Littlejohn
7. Hall, Hogan, Henshaw, Zimmerman
8. Talbot, Foster, Kirkland, Glasser
9. Benedict, Wright, Gibson, McKenna
10. Morgan, Love, Kawalski, Botnick

26. TRIPLE PLAY

1. Name Millie and Jerry Helper's three children.
2. At various times, Ethel Mertz was given three different middle names. Do you recall them?
3. Name the three chimpanzees who costarred with Peggy Cass and Jack Weston on *The Hathaways*.
4. Ves Painter, Cody Bristol, and E. J. Stocker were his rodeo pals. Who was he?
5. What three similar roles did Bernadette Withers play on *Bachelor Father*?
6. Name Steve Douglas's triplet grandsons.
7. Who won three Emmys in 1956?
8. Name the three series in which Sally Field starred.
9. What show featured Alvin, Simon, and Theodore?
10. Name the three children on *The Donna Reed Show*.

27. WHICH CAME FIRST

Select the program with the earliest premiere date from each group.

1. a) *Getting Together*, b) *The Courtship of Eddie's Father*, c) *Broadside*
2. a) *SurfSide 6*, b) *Peyton Place*, c) *The F.B.I.*
3. a) *Honestly, Celeste*, b) *Mr. Peepers*, c) *You'll Never Get Rich*
4. a) *Everybody's Talking*, b) *What's My Line?*, c) *To Tell the Truth*
5. a) *The First Hundred Years*, b) *The Guiding Light*, c) *Search for Tomorrow*
6. a) *Howdy Doody*, b) *Captain Video and His Video Rangers*, c) *Captain Kangaroo*
7. a) *Gunsmoke*, b) *Maverick*, c) *The Roy Rogers Show*
8. a) *The Texaco Star Theatre*, b) *Toast of the Town*, c) *Calvacade of Stars*
9. a) *Riverboat*, b) *Yancy Derringer*, c) *Route 66*
10. a) *Judd for the Defense*, b) *Perry Mason*, c) *The Defenders*

28. "KUKLA, FRAN AND OLLIE"

1. What was Ollie's full name, where was he born, and at what school was he educated?
2. What was Madame Ooglepuss's first name?
3. Who was Madame's Southern gentleman friend?
4. Who answered the Kuklapolitan's fan mail?
5. Can you recall the show's opening theme song?
6. Who created the show?
7. What did Buelah [sic] Witch shout as she came in for a landing?
8. Which puppet character had a speech problem which resulted in every word being "tooie"?
9. Who flew in from the North Pole regularly to pester Ollie?
10. Describe Mercedes.

29. BOOB TUBERS

1. Where was *The Addams Family* home located?
2. How big was Oliver and Lisa Douglas's farm?
3. Where did *The Aldrich Family* live?
4. *America After Dark* became what famous show?
5. Name the first host on *The Midnight Special*.
6. Where did Annie Oakley live?
7. Who was Arthur Godfrey's announcer?
8. Whom did Mike Douglas marry on *My Three Sons*?
9. Who narrated *Bat Masterson*?
10. Name the program that Robert Ripley hosted in the early fifties.

30. TV FIRSTS

1. Who was the first black performer to win an Emmy?
2. What was the first cartoon series specifically produced for television?
3. What was the first TV serial?
4. What was the first dramatic series filmed in color?
5. When was the first boxing match televised?
6. Who was Johnny Carson's first guest on the *Tonight* show?
7. Who was the first guest on *This Is Your Life*?
8. Who appeared first as Joe Friday's partner on *Dragnet*?
9. When did Mike Stokey first present *Pantomime Quiz*?
10. Who was the first Emmy winner as "Outstanding Personality"?

31. NAME, PLEASE

Provide last names for these characters.

1. Alice—*The Brady Bunch*
2. Luigi—*Life With Luigi*
3. Potsie—*Happy Days*
4. Willy—*Mission: Impossible*
5. Logo—*How to Marry a Millionaire*
6. Ethel and Albert—*Ethel and Albert*
7. Vi—*Private Secretary*
8. Aunt Harriet—*Batman*
9. Cricket—*Hawaiian Eye*
10. Whitey—*Leave It to Beaver*

32. PLACE SETTINGS

Match the locale with its program.

1. New Orleans
2. Scott Island
3. Goose Bar Ranch in Wyoming
4. Skagway, Alaska
5. Collinsport, Maine
6. Mapleton
7. San Pedro, California
8. Isola
9. Wretched, Colorado
10. Miami Beach

a. *SurfSide 6*
b. *Yancy Derringer*
c. *Dark Shadows*
d. *Waterfront*
e. *Harbourmaster*
f. *My Friend Flicka*
g. *87th Precinct*
h. *Pistols 'n' Petticoats*
i. *The Alaskans*
j. *The World of Mr. Sweeney*

33. CHANNEL CHARMERS

1. For what newspaper did Tim *(My Favorite Martian)* O'Hara work as a reporter?

2. Who played Captain Midnight, and what was the name of his spaceship?

3. Roxanne was a beautiful blonde game show assistant during the 1950s. What was her real name?

4. What was Opie Taylor's friend Johnny Paul's last name?

5. What did *Your First Impression* and *It Could Be You* have in common?

6. Name the O.K. Oil Company president who purchased the Clampett property in the Ozarks.

7. Dodge City blacksmith Quint Asper was a half-breed. Name his mother's tribe.

8. At what college was Hank Dearborn a "drop in"?

9. Name the baby born to Betty Jo and Steve Elliott on *Petticoat Junction*.

10. What was Edith Bunker's maiden name?

34. WHO . . .

1. . . . was known as "The Bronx Boswell"?
2. . . . played Joan Davis's father on *I Married Joan?*
3. . . . . created puppets Dizzy Lou and Hey You, Jack Webbfoot, Moon Mad Tiger, Marilyn Mongrel, Tearalong the Dotted Lion, and Louie the Lone Shark?
4. . . . played these *Superman* roles: Mortimer Murray, Legs Lemmy, Si Horton, and Arnold Woodman?
5. . . . hosted *Climax!?*
6. . . . was known as the "Waukegan Wit"?
7. . . . was the sportswriter on *Dear Phoebe?*
8. . . . was Corliss Archer's boyfriend?
9. . . . played the nightclub owner on *Acapulco?*
10. . . . ran the *Actor's Hotel?*

35. A GAME OF JACKS

1. Who hosted the early game show *I've Got News for You?*

2. Benny Rubin and Frank Nelson were two of his favorite comedy foils. Who was he?

3. Between Audrey Meadows and Sheila MacRae, another actress portrayed Alice Kramden in Jackie Gleason's *Honeymooners* sketches. Who was she?

4. What was Jack Paar's opening theme song on the *Tonight* show?

5. With what variety show host would you associate Don Ameche, Kitty Kallen, and Constance Towers?

6. Name Jack LaLanne's canine assistants.

7. Jack Linkletter hosted an ABC musical series filmed on various college campuses. Name it.

8. Jack Barry's *Winky Dink and You* featured what dog?

9. Who hosted *You're in the Picture?*

10. Who played John Dehner's secretary at *Today's World* magazine on *The Doris Day Show?*

36. THE YEAR 1951

Identify the television programs from these *TV Guide* capsule descriptions.

1. Bud Collyer and Roxanne coach time-racing contestants who vie for prizes.

2. Sherman Billingsley chats with well-known personalities from society, the arts, and industry.

3. Frankie Thomas has interplanetary adventures when Orion goes to Mars.

4. People tell TV audiences why they need money, and receive gifts via sponsors' phone calls and "The Helping Hand."

5. Ray Heatherton has a magic postbox.

6. He gags and ad-libs, complete with cigar.

7. Darren McGavin is the crewcut cameraman.

8. Homer causes Henry to miss an important dinner date.

9. The girls want to go to a nightclub, but Fred has other ideas.

10. Calhoun gives Andy some bad legal advice.

37. THE YEAR 1952

Identify the television programs from these *TV Guide* capsule descriptions.

1. Games, stories, and prizes for youngsters with Midnight the Cat, and Squeekie the Mouse.

2. Clifton Fadiman runs TV's clinic for performers with problems. Permanent panelists include George S. Kaufman and Sam Levenson.

3. Neil Hamilton appears with aspirants who hope to make Hollywood their next stop.

4. Louise Beavers in the role of the Hendersons' maid.

5. Pete Ball mistakes some vichysoisse for a pot of wallpaper paste.

6. Martha Scott and Pinky Lee in a situation song-and-dance series.

7. Jack Barry and his high-I.Q. moppets.

8. A jail-breaker is out to get Mike Barnett for sending him up the river.

9. Jerry and Pam invite Lt. Bill Weigand for a weekend visit to help solve the homicide of a beautiful blonde.

10. Biff and Louise become involved with an escaped American flier.

38. THE YEAR 1953

Identify the television programs from these *TV Guide* capsule descriptions.

1. Jack comes to her mother's rescue when June discovers she is wearing the same outfit as an influential member of a country club.
2. The family is horrified when they think Randolph may be a coward.
3. Octogenarians solve viewers' problems. Jack Barry emcees.
4. Liz Cooper's cousin pays her a visit but rapidly wears out her welcome.
5. Commander Swift is kidnapped by a gang of interplanetary credit-unit counterfeiters.
6. Dave's special guest is harpist Elaine Vito, a member of resident Skitch Henderson's orchestra.
7. Doc Allison almost finds himself heading a private banking institution when Jeep opens a special checking account.
8. Elliott must get inside the Kremlin to contact an unknown man in order to stop the use of a deadly weapon.
9. Contestants try to identify a face from their past. Jack Smith emcees.
10. The entire family pitches in to help Dagmar prepare for her first military ball.

39. THE YEAR 1954

Identify the television programs from these *TV Guide* capsule descriptions.

1. Henrietta plans a modest wedding for her niece, but it grows into a mammoth affair, and Cosmo sees himself faced with bankruptcy.
2. "Honest Albie" is the nickname Albie doesn't get as judge of the flower show. Seems the winning chrysanthemums belong to Albie's wife Catherine.
3. Russell Hayden, Jackie Coogan, and Phil Arnold star in the stories of western government agents, post-Civil War to 1900, in their efforts to bring law and order to the West.
4. Kirby Grant in the title role with Gloria Winters as Penny.
5. Robinson and Nancy stop off at his mother's house for a rest before they return to summer school.
6. Comrade Herb, FBI counterspy, has a close call when the Reds test his Party loyalty.
7. Songs, music, and comedy with Don McNeill as toastmaster and Fran "Aunt Fanny" Allison.
8. Jack Barry with more crayon projects for young viewers.
9. Raymond Wallace lands in hot water when he helps a lovesick laundress.
10. As a regular Thursday feature, an engaged couple will get a chance to win a wedding gown.

40. THE YEAR 1955

Identify the television programs from these *TV Guide* capsule descriptions.

1. "Buzz" learns some strange things about solids, liquids, and gases from Don Herbert.
2. Dr. Wilson invites his neighbor, Donald Peterson, on a fishing trip and learns an important lesson in psychology.
3. Steve inherits some money and in the fine old tradition of "share and share alike," Denny and Earl proceed to spend it.
4. Investigation leads Lieutenant Guthrie and Inspector Grebb to suspect that girls are responsible for a group of tavern robberies.
5. Senator Bourke B. Hickenlooper is queried by Washington youngsters. Stephen McCormick moderates.
6. Art Baker introduces film shots of the treatment for psychoneurotic racehorses, and of Merv Taylor, a movie stuntman.
7. Captain Scuttlebutt tricks Dilly into giving up his job.
8. "To join or not to join" is supposedly the question when Mrs. Bronson is invited to join Mrs. Boone's club.
9. Bob thinks that the latest candidate for city council would be an ideal candidate for sister Margaret's hand.
10. Captain John tries to help a boy who has learned his father is a criminal.

41. THE YEAR 1956

Identify the television programs from these *TV Guide* capsule descriptions.

1. Tagg's ventriloquism comes in handy when a young rancher refuses to testify against his outlaw brother.
2. Tim and Toubo are hired to track down a killer whale who threatens to destroy many fishing craft.
3. A prominent sculptress wants to rent a house from the Thackery Realty Company.
4. Host Jack Douglas interviews Hettie Dyhrnfurth, who holds the world's mountain-climbing record for women.
5. A neighbor of the Millers thinks that children are a nuisance, and puts a barbed-wire fence around his property to keep Jeff and Porky out.
6. Nephew Rodney is fired from the Racquet Club staff.
7. Dick Powell introduces Lee J. Cobb, who stars in "Death Watch."
8. Ken's father and the rest of the small ranch owners in the valley wonder who is ruining the grazing land.
9. Matt Anders discovers a direct connection between the theft of stimulants and several trucking accidents.
10. After a monkey begins losing his teeth, Noah and Sam decide to experiment with a new dental transplant method.

42. THE YEAR 1957

Identify the television programs from these *TV Guide* capsule descriptions.

1. Ringmaster Jack Sterling introduces circus acts, acrobats, and others.//
2. Edward Everett Horton guest stars as a butler lent to the Henshaws by Matt's boss, who is vacationing in Europe.
3. Mike Barnes journeys to Budapest at the time of the Hungarian revolution to help the press-service bureau chief escape.
4. Barbara, who feels she is always in the background because of her famous sister Margaret, decides to become a professional singer.
5. Cochise learns of Geronimo's plan to attack Fort Grant.
6. Liza Hammond returns home from her lecture tour to find her household in an uproar.
7. Howard and Eve are all set to appear in a monumental production of *The Taming of the Shrew*.
8. Nick and Nora recall how they met with the help of a puppy.
9. The judge uncovers a plot to steal the Indian's land.
10. When Jane comes home with a new silk dress, Dick hits the ceiling.

43. THE YEAR 1958

Identify the television programs from these *TV Guide* capsule descriptions.

1. Rip Masters buys Red Eagle, a horse he believes will win the jumping competitions between Fort Apache and Fort Comanche.

2. When a young Texan's oil tanker runs aground, Bullwinkle sees a chance to profit by the disaster.

3. Luke meets with opposition at home when he tells Grandpa that he wants to get a job in town working evenings.

4. Bentley decides to send Kelly to a girls' finishing school so that she will acquire some polish.

5. Mike is hired to salvage a German submarine sunk off the coast of South America.

6. Bart Grant investigates an accident which occurred years ago.

7. Sergeants Hollis and Goodrich are assigned to investigate the murder of a man who was stabbed.

8. Texas Ranger Hoby Gilman begins an investigation of a bank robber.

9. Jim Hardie tries to establish the real identity of a white boy living with an Indian tribe.

10. Lieutenant Ballinger attempts to round up a gang of dangerous teenage hoodlums at a trade school.

44. THE YEAR 1959

Identify the television programs from these *TV Guide* capsule descriptions.

1. Private detective Stuart Bailey and his partner, Jeff Spencer, are retained by a Washington attorney to protect his wife.

2. Rowdy Yates stops a runaway horse.

3. Dennis Chase is asked to investigate the death of James North.

4. Chief Marshal Simon Fry plans to help three youngsters orphaned by the murder of their parents.

5. Jody and his friends Homer and Abby decide to earn money to buy high-wheel bicycles.

6. Josh Randall is hunting a murderer in hopes of collecting the reward.

7. Grey Holden takes the *Enterprise* up river with a cargo of arms and recruits for the Fort Union outpost.

8. Johnny Yuma returns home after the truce at Appomattox and finds his father dead.

9. Captain Shafer, Chick's commanding officer, tries to arrange a romance for his attractive daughter.

10. Colonel Edward McCauley and three other men have been assigned to man the first space rocket to the moon.

45. THE YEAR 1960

Identify the television programs from these *TV Guide* capsule descriptions.

1. Car trouble lands Tod and Buzz in the out of the way town of Garth.

2. Dan Adams investigates mysterious goings-on aboard a tramp steamer.

3. Rusty has accidentally broken his dad's golf clubs, and thinks maybe things won't go so hard if he can talk Linda into taking the blame.

4. Loco tries to prevent a nightclub comedienne from destroying her romance with a rich beau.

5. Tom gives a young man advice on how to get along as a real estate salesman.

6. Katy's convinced that the only way for Olive and Dr. Gray to get married is to elope.

7. Babs takes a job as a model, but Bill and Brook don't think this is such a great idea.

8. Jeannie becomes manager of a Chinese restaurant that Al and Liz own.

9. Robbie thinks the family is out for his blood. Seems everything he does is wrong and everything Mike does is right.

10. Aunt Violet and Aunt Iris think it would be fine for their nephew to marry.

46. THE YEAR 1961

Identify the television programs from these *TV Guide* capsule descriptions.

1. The prospective in-laws finally meet when Kay's parents are invited for dinner at the Dunston mansion.

2. Wilma is tired of being taken for granted, so Fred decides he better start courting his wife all over again.

3. Skydivers Ted and Jim are accused of killing a scientist.

4. Buddy has an offer of a better job and wants out of his present contract with Mel Cooley.

5. Doctor Hyatt solves the case without the help of Corey and Sills.

6. King and Casey plan to trap a diamond-smuggling ring in South Africa.

7. In his "Dear Debbie" column, Bob advises a young couple to elope.

8. Huckabee asks Lackland to take him to a neighboring island to search for tribal masks.

9. Toody and Muldoon head the entertainment committee for the Christmas party at the precinct.

10. Maggie and Ted plan to leave the staff of County General Hospital.

47. THE YEAR 1962

Identify the television programs from these *TV Guide* capsule descriptions.

1. The Finches have agreed on the exchange plan and now all Eddie Walker has to do is tell his wife.

2. Rick and Wally are planning a dinner party for their fraternity brothers.

3. Mary's friend is getting married and the Stone family offers its home for the wedding.

4. Dana March wants Mike and Larry to recover a trophy from her sunken boat.

5. Redigo defends ranch hand Moreno, who is accused of killing a woman.

6. Lime's off to Mexico to collect a debt from a retired bullfighter.

7. Father Fitzgibbons is preparing for a visit home to Bally Moora, Ireland, but Father O'Malley protests.

8. It's Wes's birthday and Tom-Tom, Vern, and Howie have a party planned.

9. Colonel Blackwell's former commanding officer stops by Westfield to ask a favor.

10. Half-breed Quint Asper returns home to find that two white men have just shot his father.

48. THE YEAR 1963

Identify the television programs from these *TV Guide* capsule descriptions.

1. Betty Jo enters the annual Shady Rest Horseshoe Tournament.

2. Harry asks Lois to pretend she's French.

3. The Kissel kids and Jenny hop aboard the wagon train taking Doc west.

4. Katy heads for home after she and Glenn disagree.

5. A distraught father asks Neil Brock for help.

6. During his chemistry class, Maynard accidentally douses himself with a solution that seems to have a magnetic appeal for the female of the species.

7. Harry Grafton's department is thrown into a frenzy by a new electronic computer.

8. Rice is assigned to Kasten's platoon as a recruit private.

9. Chaos reigns in the Lane household because Aunt Pauline is due for a visit.

10. Eddie wants Jose to pretend he's the hotel manager.

49. THE YEAR 1964

Identify the television programs from these *TV Guide* capsule descriptions.

1. To get an exclusive story, Danny offers to hide an informer from the gunmen who are seeking revenge.
2. The murder of an official at a nuclear power plant leads Solo and Illya to suspect someone is trying to get fissionable material.
3. Captain Binghamton wants to ship Parker off to a lookout station on a deserted island.
4. Betty tries to break up Rodney's date with Allison, and Constance confides to Swain that she's unhappy.
5. Sam charters the *Island Princess* to a city official for a day of fishing.
6. At one of his subsidiary companies, Walter is mistaken for an employee.
7. Regulars Nancy Ames, Phyllis Newman, David Frost, Buck Henry, Bob Dishy, and Pat Englund celebrate the holidays by roasting a few chestnuts in the news.
8. Jimmy O'Neill welcomes the New Beats, Jackie and Gayle, and regulars Donna Loren and Bobby Sherman.
9. Owen Sharpe suggests replacing the whole complaint department with a computer named I.R.M.A.
10. Will joins the Air Police so he won't have to leave his dog Blue.

50. THE YEAR 1965

Identify the television programs from these *TV Guide* capsule descriptions.

1. Apprentice angel Tom is sent to a hobo jungle in search of an unpublished author.
2. On special orders, Commander Talbot's destroyer heads for Norway to pick up British commandos.
3. Enterprising Hank's latest business venture is date-making on campus.
4. The new swimming pool creates quite a splash, so the girls at Camp Divine decide to have some fun.
5. Varner learns that Ben Quick needs a bank loan to rebuild his farm.
6. In Hong Kong, Kelly receives sealed orders from Russ Conley, a colleague.
7. Maureen manages to reach John, who is drifting helplessly in space.
8. As a favor to his Indian friends, O'Rourke plans to smuggle a cannon out of the fort.
9. Although Jim and Joan can't act or sing, they agreed to perform in a school play.
10. Saunders and his men feel more like camp counselors than soldiers when they are assigned four teen-age replacements.

51. THE YEAR 1966

Identify the television programs from these *TV Guide* capsule descriptions.

1. Tony and Doug are taken to a 1910 mining town.

2. A trading post worker plans to make some quick cash by stealing Jai's pet leopard.

3. Ann has a chance to join Jules Benedict's acting workshop if she can impress him at the audition.

4. Bill tries to cure Cissy's hero worship for her high school psychology teacher.

5. Shepperd, Gage, and André must destroy a German submarine.

6. A well-digger finds water for Haney—by tapping Oliver's well.

7. Dave and Julie are frantically trying to earn some extra money to buy furniture.

8. Jim Ed Love hires the world's best cowboy to show Ben and Howdy what cowpunching really means.

9. McCullough is astonished when Paul Bryan informs him that Diana is alive.

10. Hitchcock is wounded and Troy is determined to take him to the nearest aid station, a German field hospital.

52. THE YEAR 1967

Identify the television programs from these *TV Guide* capsule descriptions.

1. Sandy and Tracy enter their pet lambs in a farm fair contest.

2. A rare allergy robs Endora of her powers, which mysteriously switch to Aunt Clara.

3. In London, Lee Bailey visits the home of Sean Connery and his wife.

4. Paula and Dick try to aid and comfort their fireman friend Harry.

5. Drake joins a mercenary army to investigate a plot against a newly independent African agent.

6. Detectives Haines, Ward, and Corso go after a sniper who tried to assassinate a visiting V.I.P.

7. Doctor Tracy dispatches a search party for Judy.

8. In a besieged Belgian village, Gallagher and Komansky search for a way to translate captured Luftwaffe documents.

9. Sajid Khan as orphan boy Raji befriends an American boy in a local village.

10. Edwin and Luke are a couple of sad dads. Each believes that the other has only six months to live.

53. THE YEAR 1968

Identify the television programs from these *TV Guide* capsule descriptions.

1. Will and Jeff encounter Billy Delver on the trail.
2. Mark searches deep in the Everglades for a swamp tramp.
3. A routine case soon has David Ross embroiled in murder.
4. Young Corey has a disturbing question: is Santa Claus black or white?
5. Johnny Carson trades quips with Don tonight, with Pat McCormick and the Vic Mizzy orchestra.
6. Police captain Fomento, San Juan's answer to Inspector Clouseau, investigates a convent bazaar.
7. Rufus and Bert prepare to make a TV commercial for the diner.
8. Mundy must retrieve stolen scrolls that have a unifying effect on an emerging African nation.
9. Eve and Kaye help save Jerry's job at a computer-dating service.
10. Robert Dickson and Gloria Quigley marry.

54. THE YEAR 1969

Identify the television programs from these *TV Guide* capsule descriptions.

1. Intense competition leads to possible tragedy for starlets Diane and Rachel.

2. Jeff Dillon gets involved in a bizarre case when a D.A. gives him a phony story.

3. Israel uses all his backwoods ingenuity to help a runaway elude his pursuers.

4. The Gull Cottage crew tries to rescue an errant seal.

5. An old Army buddy of Sam's makes a play for Millie.

6. Chet finds himself facing an irate school counselor.

7. Scott and Bob nurse a wolf wounded by a hunter.

8. Buck and Manolito wheel and deal to buy a ranch laden with silver.

9. Malloy and Reed fight interference while arresting an injured burglary suspect.

10. Counselor Liz McIntyre goes out of her way to help embittered student Jason Allen.

55. THE YEAR 1970

Identify the television programs from these *TV Guide* capsule descriptions.

1. Greg and Marcia get their first chance to babysit for their younger brothers and sisters.

2. Dr. Goldstone tries to save the hospital's free clinic.

3. Adam suffers a severe case of carat complex while shopping for Nancy's engagement ring.

4. Gannon tries to save a sixteen-year-old patient from heroin addiction.

5. Norman gives the Corbetts a special gift.

6. Aaron and Pat reopen a murder case.

7. Marlin Perkins tangles with a giant octopus.

8. Andy calls a meeting with parents in hopes of bridging the generation gap.

9. Linc feigns insanity to gain admittance to a mental institution.

10. Honey Robinson sends the newlyweds to his hot-shot cousin to buy a bed wholesale.

56. THE YEAR 1971

Identify the television programs from these *TV Guide* capsule descriptions.

1. Hank Brackett and Johnny Reach lend assistance to a Mexican revolution.
2. Heyes and Curry have trouble evading a local sheriff.
3. The murder of a prostitute forces Father Cavanaugh into a painful investigation.
4. Chad and Betty miss the children at Christmas. With Ron Howard.
5. A capricious corpse that won't stay put leads Crooke and Robinson on a slapstick search.
6. Shirley is in Hong Kong keen on promoting the fortunes of a hapless Jewish cab driver and a rock star.
7. Keith falls in love with a girl auditioning for the group.
8. Law-and-order is the topic and our five couples get a chance to create their own when stranded on a desert island.
9. Reta Shaw plays a maid who takes over the Nuvo home, lock, stock and menu (she's serving buffalo kidneys tonight).
10. Arlo and J.J. get themselves into trouble in Madrid County.

PHOTO ANALYSIS

1. What subject did Mr. Peepers teach?

ANSWERS FOR PHOTO QUIZ APPEAR ON PAGE 154

2. What did Garry Moore call the news portion of his morning variety show?

3. Where did the Andersons live?

4. Where did Margie and Vern Albright live?

5. What was the call-in telephone number on *Ted Mack's Original Amateur Hour*?

6. With what TV personality would you associate this performer, and who is she?

7. What was Kookie's full name?

8. Who created the *Today* program?

57. THE YEAR 1972

Identify the television programs from these *TV Guide* capsule descriptions.

1. Jake Webster, undercover agent, is after an escaped con bent on revenge.
2. Grover would rather lead the life of a playboy than follow Cameron's instructions.
3. Doctor Campanelli threatens to quit.
4. The Steinbergs have won an audience with the Pope and the Fitzgeralds have tickets to Israel.
5. Doctor Jamison's peskiest patient just got himself trapped in a mine shaft.
6. Fran Belding is on a mailing list of future murder victims.
7. A horrible death awaits Glenn Garth Gregory as he tries to unravel the mystery of a prisoner on an island.
8. Mamie and Emily have their eyes on Grandpa.
9. Jefferson Keyes helps a tycoon facing a murder conviction.
10. Howie and Barbara take pity on a mugger and bring him home to dinner.

58. THE YEAR 1973

Identify the television programs from these *TV Guide* capsule descriptions.

1. Amanda's defending a porno movie theater owner while Adam is prosecuting him.

2. Someone sneaked a peek at Nathan's favorite dress design and sold it to his arch rival.

3. John is trying to hide Sally's birthday present from her divining powers.

4. Fusco insists on going out on Balukis's date with Joe.

5. Walter's plans for "I Love You Day" are foundering in the tears of newly divorced Vivian Cavender.

6. Is Stanley about to get rid of his slovenly brother-in-law or is it just another futile dream?

7. Caine sets out to recover a golden chalice stolen from a mission then lost to outlaws.

8. Anthony Blake tries to solve the murder of his best friend.

9. Steve and Mike try to break a syndicate numbers racket.

10. Jed and Sweet disagree over the use of the platoon jeep.

59. THE YEAR 1974

Identify the television programs from these *TV Guide* capsule descriptions.

1. A feisty fourteen-year-old is making life miserable for Sonny and Will on the road.

2. Moze enters Addie in a small-town Shirley Temple talent contest.

3. Florida is on the rampage, and her bewildered family is at a loss to explain her irritability.

4. Mama is practicing her matchmaking skills by trying to set up Clifton with a girlfriend.

5. The Adamsons must deal with a marauding killer leopard menacing the compound.

6. Ryker and Terry are trapped at headquarters by a crooked ex-cop.

7. A quiet Christmas at the Bellamy house goes awry when two new arrivals at Eaton Place disappear.

8. Rocky tries to help his son solve a year-long investigation.

9. As a tornado approaches Lamont, Truckie takes the kids while Zack and Doobie are trapped together in the basement.

10. Jeff's confused and concerned when his mother begins to display a coolness toward his girlfriend Anita.

60. THE YEAR 1975

Identify the television programs from these *TV Guide* capsule descriptions.

1. A smitten Bang Bang persuades Eddie to hire a maid.

2. The Hartleys play host to a group of patients.

3. Tony is infuriated to hear folk music during mass, and Rose is upset about his outburst in church.

4. The officers become keenly aware of public hostility toward policemen after Yemana is shot by ambushers and bystanders refuse to help.

5. Joe takes on a masher at the Gerards' first anniversary dinner.

6. A glory-hungry police lieutenant hinders Pepper and Crowley as they search for the person who killed a policeman.

7. Joe worries when he learns that Mark is dating the daughter of a woman with a bad reputation.

8. Gabe persuades Vinnie to run for the office of president of the student body.

9. Howard asks Richie to entertain the daughter of a visiting businessman.

10. Ann causes a crisis by refusing to allow sixteen-year-old Julie to go on a boy-girl camping trip.

61. THE YEAR 1976

Identify the television programs from these *TV Guide* capsule descriptions.

1. Merle Jeeter locks Loretta in his motel room.

2. Cass's plane has been hijacked and the only clue is a jumbled radio message Stan believes is in code.

3. Walter Franklin finds that hiring a law clerk can be a trying experience.

4. Sam Casey pits his power of invisibility against the destructive force of a computerized robot.

5. Jamie poses as a female wrestler while trying to pin down a lead on a missing O.S.I. agent.

6. The Baudine brothers are taken captive by a band of ruthless buffalo hunters.

7. It's Barton versus Plunkett as the two pitchers hurl practical jokes at each other.

8. An airport sneak thief seeks Pete and Mac's help when a stolen attache case reveals a bundle of money.

9. Charley bares the details of her relationship with Richard in a magazine article.

10. George flatly refuses to attend Lionel's wedding.

62. THE YEAR 1977

Identify the television programs from these *TV Guide* capsule descriptions.

1. Chief Roy's plans for a fishing trip flounder when he finds out his backwoods buddy is homosexual.
2. Lenny fumes at friends he holds responsible for a fire that gutted his apartment.
3. A full moon produces a string of strange cases in night court, and gets Matt into a crazy lover's quarrel with Maureen.
4. Mark swims through an undersea rift into 14th-century Verona.
5. Judy's innocent luncheon date with an old boyfriend proves too great a test for Stuart's sense of security.
6. The *Sea Tiger*'s chance to sink an enemy tanker may be torpedoed when Sherman is stricken with appendicitis.
7. The Thorpes take on an injured man who claims to be the sole survivor of an Indian massacre.
8. A severe thunderstorm sets Ben roaming the countryside while Adams repairs the damage to his cabin.
9. Incensed when Mel hires a waiter for more money than they're making, Flo and Vera turn in their uniforms.
10. Joyce tries to cheer up a blue Mitzi who feels her career is humdrum compared to the glamorous show-biz life of her roommate.

63. THE NAME BEHIND THE DAME

Match the "old" names with the "new" names.

1. Josephine Owaissa Cottle
2. Frances Octavia Smith
3. Barbara Brantingham
4. Patricia Neal
5. Margone Chandler
6. Margaret Theresa Yvonne Reed
7. Peggy Middleton
8. Ruby Stevens
9. Susan Miller
10. Donna Mae Jaden

a. Susan St. James
b. Janis Paige
c. Gale Storm
d. Fannie Flagg
e. Martha Raye
f. Dale Evans
g. Barbara Stanwyck
h. Yvonne DeCarlo
i. Dorothy Collins
j. Barbara Britton

64. TELEQUIZ

1. Who was "King of the Wild Stallions"?
2. Name Thorny Thornberry's wife.
3. What was James West's *(The Wild, Wild West)* birthdate?
4. What is Radar O'Reilly's hometown?
5. What are the CB "handles" of Starsky and Hutch?
6. What are the first names of Archie Bunker's parents?
7. On *The Life of Riley*, who was Annie Riley?
8. Who was Sam Jones's girlfriend on *Mayberry, R.F.D.*?
9. Name Heath Barkley's horse.
10. What is Fred the Cockatoo's real name?

65. MENAGERIE MATCH

Match the animal with the show on which he appeared.

1. Aristotle
2. Useless
3. Ulysses
4. Bimbo
5. Scar
6. Bruce
7. Pete
8. Hank
9. Loco
10. Cinders

a. *Honey West*
b. *Cisco Kid*
c. *The Addams Family*
d. *Casey Jones*
e. *Circus Boy*
f. *Hotel de Paree*
g. *Pistols 'n' Petticoats*
h. *Flipper*
i. *Restless Gun*
j. *Iron Horse*

66. SCHOOL DAYS

1. Where did Professor McNulty teach?

2. Where was Mingo *(Daniel Boone)* educated?

3. With what school subject would you associate teacher Dione Lucas?

4. Who was Madison High's *(Our Miss Brooks)* star football player?

5. Who took over as principal at Jefferson High School after Dean Jagger left the *Mr. Novak* cast?

6. What was Mr. Kaufman's first name on *Room 222*?

7. Who was Joey Newton's *(Fury)* school teacher?

8. Whose classmate was know-it-all Judy Hensler?

9. "Uncle Martin" came to earth as a professor of what subject?

10. At what school was Stu Erwin principal?

67. CLOSED CIRCUIT

1. Who danced with Bobby Burgess on *The Lawrence Welk Show* before Cissy King?

2. What familiar melody was employed for the *Howdy Doody* theme song?

3. Who was Samantha Stephens's warlock physician?

4. Name the museum where Captain Kangaroo acts as a keeper.

5. What is Chin Ho's last name?

6. What mid-fifties character did svelte Irish McCalla play?

7. Who taught at Mrs. Nestor's Private School for Girls?

8. On *Mr. Peepers*, what was Nancy Remington's father's name?

9. Name the series in which Gary Merrill and William Prince played brothers and attorneys.

10. Who played the French teacher on *Our Miss Brooks*?

68. VARIETY'S SPICE

Furnish the program or personality with whom you would associate each group of variety show performers.

1. Snowflake, Paul Lynde, Lisa Kirk, Mitchell Ayres Orchestra

2. Bambi Linn and Rod Alexander, The Bob Hamilton Trio, The Billy Williams Quartet, Cliff Norton

3. Kevin Carlisle Dancers, Harry Zimmerman Orchestra, George Beckerman Singers, Dorothy Loudon

4. Tony Charmoli Dancers, Johnny Mann Singers, Paul Weston Orchestra, Harvey Korman

5. Nick Castle Dancers, George Wyle Singers, Lou Brown Orchestra, Osmond Brothers

6. Louis DaPron Dancers, Jimmy Joyce Singers, Nelson Riddle Orchestra, Pat Paulsen

7. Quincy Jones Orchestra, Foster Brooks, Donald McKayle Dancers, Susan Tolsky

8. Pat Carroll, The Sauter-Finegan Orchestra, Danny Hoctor and Betty Byrd, Hy Averback

9. Herb Ross Dancers, Charlie Applegate, Allen Roth Orchestra, Jack Lescoulie

10. David Rose Orchestra, The Tom Hanson Dancers, Alan Copeland Singers, Art Gilmore

69. NAMELY

Furnish the first names of these characters.

1. Markham—*Markham*
2. Mr. Canaday—*Bonanza*
3. Potsie—*Happy Days*
4. Doc McPheeters—*The Travels of Jaime McPheeters*
5. Fish—*Barney Miller*
6. Thorny—*The Adventures of Ozzie and Harriet*
7. Mr. Sweeney—*The World of Mr. Sweeney*
8. Darby—*The Adventures of Ozzie and Harriet*
9. LeBeau—*Hogan's Heroes*
10. "Stretch" Cunningham—*All in the Family*

70. "HOWDY DOODY"

1. What was Clarabell's full name?
2. True or false: Clarabell never spoke on TV.
3. How many freckles on Howdy's face?
4. Who was John J. Fedoozle?
5. What was Howdy's flying machine called?
6. Name at least three *Howdy Doody* sponsors.
7. How did Clarabell communicate?
8. Who was the old, salty sea captain?
9. Who was the storekeeper in Doodyville?
10. Who played Princess Summerfall Winterspring?

71. PRIME TIME

1. Who were Bruce Podewell and Susan Levin?

2. Name the Goldberg's favorite mountain resort.

3. Where did Lois Lane live?

4. Where did Pearson Norby work?

5. Carl Sandburg called him "a reporter, historian, inquirer, actor, ponderer, and seeker." To whom was the poet referring?

6. Name the host of *Down You Go,* who also wrote most of the queries used on *The $64,000 Question*.

7. His supporting cast included Doris Drew, Skip Farrell, Molly Bee, and Jack Fascinato. Name the performer.

8. On what show was *No Time for Sergeants* first presented?

9. This classic character of literature was played by Ronald Howard and his aide by H. Marion Crawford. Name the series.

10. Who played Eddie Mayehoff's wife on *That's My Boy?*

72. TRAINS & BOATS & PLANES

Match the vehicle with the show in which it was featured.

1. Fortuna
2. Songbird
3. Enterprise
4. Jupiter II
5. Minnow
6. Amsterdam Queen
7. Cheryl Ann
8. Seaview
9. Polaris
10. Cannonball

a. Sky King
b. Mr. Lucky
c. Voyage to the Bottom of the Sea
d. Tom Corbett, Space Cadet
e. Petticoat Junction
f. Gilligan's Island
g. Waterfront
h. Lost in Space
i. Riverboat
j. The Queen and I

73. GIRL GAMES

Match the actress with the game show with which you would associate her.

1. Lynn Dollar
2. Janice Gilbert
3. Connie Carroll
4. Evelyn Patrick
5. Carolyn Stroupe
6. Roxanne
7. Jackie Loughery
8. Lillian Naud
9. Carol Merrill
10. Janis Carter

a. *The Big Surprise*
b. *The $64,000 Question*
c. *Feather Your Nest*
d. *Haggis Baggis*
e. *Earn Your Vacation*
f. *Let's Make a Deal*
g. *Stop the Music*
h. *Beat the Clock*
i. *Dollar a Second*
j. *Break the Bank*

74. WHO'S IN CHARGE HERE?

Match the employer with the series in which the character was featured.

1. Mr. Fuddy
2. Mr. Thackery
3. J. B. Hafter
4. Anson Foster
5. Commander Darwin
6. James Devery
7. Hamilton Majors
8. Peter Sands
9. Dr. Craig
10. Adam Henshaw

a. *Arnie*
b. *My Hero*
c. *A Date With the Angels*
d. *Private Secretary*
e. *The Ann Sothern Show*
f. *Life With Elizabeth*
g. *Mr. Adams and Eve*
h. *Hazel*
i. *Grindl*
j. *Lancelot Link, Secret Chimp*

75. TUNE IN

1. A regular feature of *The Garry Moore Show* was "That Wonderful Year." The finish of it was always the same—the cast would line up and sing a question. What was it?

2. Sing the sign-off theme of *Your Hit Parade*.

3. Who composed "This Is Today," the *Today* show theme?

4. Who sang "The Ballad of Johnny Yuma," theme of *The Rebel*?

5. "Oriental Blues" by Newlon was the theme for what popular comedy?

6. According to the theme song, who was "the man who flies around like an eagle"?

7. Who sang the *I Married Joan* theme song?

8. What song did "The Three Haircuts" sing on Sid Caesar's show?

9. They sang of him "in manor house, on riverboat and now and then in jail." Who was he?

10. Who sang the *Wyatt Earp* theme?

76. "BATMAN" BADDIES

Who played these villains on the popular series?

1. The Mad Hatter
2. The Joker
3. The Riddler
4. The Penguin
5. King Tut
6. Catwoman
7. Mr. Freeze
8. The Archer
9. Egghead
10. Ma Parker

77. VIDEO VERSION

1. When did Harry S. Truman make his first network TV appearance?

2. In between *Davy Crockett* and *Daniel Boone*, Fess Parker starred on an unsuccessful TV series. Name it.

3. What was the name of the song Ernie Kovacs used during his famous "Nairobi Trio" sessions?

4. On *Hogan's Heroes*, to what did "Papa Bear" and "Goldilocks" refer?

5. When did cigarette commercials on TV end?

6. Who was the auctioneer on the Lucky Strike commercials?

7. What company sponsored *The Children's Hour?*

8. How were Rusty's *(Rin Tin Tin)* parents killed?

9. What was Morticia Addams's maiden name?

10. What part did Kevin Coughlin play on *Mama?*

78. CHARACTER ANALYSIS

For each television series, two characters are furnished. Match them.

1. *The Ghost and Mrs. Muir*
2. *That Girl*
3. *The Corner Bar*
4. *December Bride*
5. *The Mothers-in-Law*
6. *Here We Go Again*
7. *Hey, Landlord!*
8. *Nancy*
9. *Petticoat Junction*
10. *Love on a Rooftop*

a. Richard Evans
b. Jerry Bauman
c. Stan Parker
d. Adam Hudson
e. Jack Ellenhorn
f. Hilda Crocker
g. Daniel Gregg
h. Roger Buell
i. Abby Townsend
j. Steve Elliott
k. Julie Willis
l. Charley Pratt
m. Susan Standish
n. Meyer Shapiro
o. Woody Banner
p. Herb Hubbard
q. Peter Porter
r. Judy Bessimer
s. Phil Bracken
t. Norrie Coolidge

80

79. SOAP BOX

Can you identify the soap operas from these *TV Guide* descriptions?

1. Tate tells Walsh of his affection for Patty.
2. Meg and Vanessa come to a showdown.
3. Dr. Corey's insight goes a lot further than a boy's second sight.
4. Jim learns that Dick is unaware of Kathy's decision to remain home.
5. Aunt Emily meets the mysterious Sandra for the first time.
6. Roy Withers has used Kim as a decoy to bring Bonnie to him.
7. Vince Bannister goes back to Nel, the Fortune Teller, to set a trap for Bill Morgan.
8. Amelia insists that Portia's son be sent out of town for the duration of the trial.
9. Maggie and Jim witness Kit's breakdown.
10. Robinson and John listen with misgivings to Lorna's story of the shooting.

80. SALES PITCH

What products are identified with the following slogans?

1. "Ah'm lazy, too lazy for pin curls."
2. "Take hospital-tested ——— and feel good again."
3. "Remember, you can be sure if it's ———."
4. "——— tastes good like a cigarette should."
5. "Only ——— has GL-70 to fight decay."
6. "Packs more pleasure because it's more perfectly packed."
7. "The modern pain reliever that acts twice as fast as aspirin."
8. "See the U.S.A. in your ———."
9. "Try it—you'll like it!"
10. "You'll whistle while you wash . . . because ——— gets out more dirt."

81. RADIOVISIONS

Match the radio performer with his or her television counterpart, and name the radio/TV program.

1. Les Damon
2. Art Baker
3. Jean VanderPyl
4. William Gargan
5. Janet Waldo
6. Brook Temple
7. Dud Williamson
8. Lon Clark
9. Hugh Marlowe
10. David Brian

a. Jack Bailey
b. Peter Lawford
c. Mark Stevens
d. Jane Wyatt
e. Art Linkletter
f. Jay Jostyn
g. Robert Conrad
h. Rocky Lane
i. George Nader
j. Ann Baker

82. ON THE AIR

1. What was Ernie's last name before he was adopted by the Douglases on *My Three Sons?*

2. Who provided the voice for *Mr. Ed?*

3. What was Steve *(Hawaii Five-O)* McGarrett's middle name?

4. Who was Kit Carson's sidekick?

5. What was Napoleon Solo's badge number?

6. What make of car did Simon Templar drive?

7. Before M*A*S*H fame, Wayne Rogers starred in a western. Name it.

8. Which sitcom ran the longest—*I Love Lucy, The Beverly Hillbillies, Father Knows Best,* or *My Three Sons?*

9. Whose afternoon show featured a fan club called the "Early Eyeball Fraternal Marching Society"?

10. Who was the announcer on *Tom Corbett, Space Cadet?*

83. "THE MARY TYLER MOORE SHOW"

1. What was the apartment number at Mary's second Minneapolis address?
2. Name the med student who broke off his romance with Mary, prompting her to move to Minneapolis.
3. On what TV channel did WJM broadcast?
4. Name the store at which Rhoda Morgenstern was employed.
5. Phyllis Lindstrom's husband Lars was a specialist in what medical field?
6. Name Mary's parents.
7. What were Murray and Lou's wives' names?
8. What was Georgette's maiden monicker?
9. Who wrote and sang the theme song "Love Is All Around"?
10. Who played Chuckles the Clown?

84. WIVES TALES

Furnish the wives' names for the husbands and programs provided.

1. Davy Crockett, *Davy Crockett*
2. Maxwell Klinger, *M*A*S*H*
3. Stanley Sowici, *You'll Never Get Rich*
4. John Gay, *Mr. and Mrs. Mystery*
5. Pearson Norby, *Norby*
6. Albie Morrison, *Pride of the Family*
7. Paul Simms, *The Paul Lynde Show*
8. Dick Preston, *The New Dick Van Dyke Show*
9. Lou Marie, *That Girl*
10. Keith Barron, *Search for Tomorrow*

85. WHO'S HE?

Match the TV character with the actor who played him.

1. Leo Schnauzer
2. Bob Wilcox
3. Casey Jones
4. Cousin Itt
5. Ripley Masters
6. Silky Harris
7. Hank Brackett
8. Boston Blackie
9. Rex Randolph
10. Cagey Calhoun

a. Felix Silla
b. Al Lewis
c. Bob Crane
d. Jesse White
e. Roger Moore
f. Kent Taylor
g. Rod Taylor
h. Richard Long
i. James L. Brown
j. Alan Hale, Jr.

86. TUBE TEST

1. He was Bob Collins's Air Force buddy and Margaret's boyfriend. Name him.

2. How many *Bicentennial Minutes* were broadcast on CBS?

3. What was the name of Groucho's duck?

4. What was June Cleaver's maiden name?

5. What TV character did both Margaret Summers and Kathy Daly marry?

6. Name Joe Friday's early-fifties girlfriend.

7. Who played The Humuhumunukunukuapuaa Kid on *Hawaiian Eye*?

8. What was Maynard G. Krebs's middle name?

9. Fill in the four missing words from these *Car 54, Where Are You?* lyrics: "There's a hold-up in The ———/Brooklyn's broken out in fights/There's a traffic jam in ——— that's backed up to Jackson Heights/There's a scout troop short a ———/Khruschev's due at ———/Car 54, Where Are You?"

10. How old was Grandpa Munster?

87. IT FIGURES

1. What was Jim Reed's badge number?

2. *The Adventures of Rin Tin Tin* followed the exploits of what cavalry?

3. What was Mr. Ed's Social Security number?

4. What was the Romano's apartment number on *One Day at a Time?*

5. How many rooms in *The Beverly Hillbillies'* mansion?

6. What was the Chicago zip code of Bob and Emily Hartley?

7. What was Adam Greer's badge number on *The Mod Squad?*

8. What was the license number of Ironside's truck?

9. What was Tony Nelson's military serial number?

10. To what platoon did Gomer Pyle belong?

88. SPOUSE IN THE HOUSE

Furnish the husband's name for the wife and program provided.

1. Elizabeth Pride, *The Road West*
2. Myrtle Davis, *Father Knows Best*
3. Angie Pallucci, *The Doris Day Show*
4. Martha McGivern, *The Californians*
5. Marjorie Grant, *Bracken's World*
6. Cora Dithers, *Blondie*
7. Alice Henderson, *Beulah*
8. Nancy Hughes, *As the World Turns*
9. Irma Boyle, *Wait Till Your Father Gets Home*
10. Debbie Thompson, *The Debbie Reynolds Show*

89. TV SCREEN TEST

1. After marrying and leaving home, Mike Douglas *(My Three Sons)* went into what profession?

2. How far did Jethro Bodine go in school?

3. What is Paul Winchell's dummy Knucklehead's last name?

4. What did Sullivan call his resident *Toast of the Town* dancers?

5. What did *Blind Date, Home,* and *Talent Patrol* have in common?

6. What was the name of the early-fifties game show which required each panelist to talk for sixty seconds on an impossible subject, such as "How to blow glass," "Zebras," and "Whale blubber"?

7. Performers included Pupi Campo, Bill and Cora Baird with their puppets, Jose Melis, and Betty Clooney. Name this daily two-hour CBS program.

8. Who constituted Milton Berle's on-screen fan club?

9. Who was Mrs. Harvey Horwich?

10. Can you identify Keegle Farven?

90. CLUB QUIZ

Identify the program whose characters belonged to these organizations.

1. The Mystic Knights of the Sea Lodge
2. The Regal Order of the Golden Door to Good Fellowship
3. The Brooklyn Patriots of Los Angeles
4. The Raccoon Lodge
5. The Grange
6. The Order of the Water Buffalo
7. The Kings of Queens
8. The Racquet Club
9. The Wednesday Afternoon Fine Arts League
10. The Sons of Norway

91. WHO'S SHE?

Match the TV character with the actress who played her.

1. Mrs. Emma Peel
2. Diana Prince
3. Holly Marshall
4. Betty Hamilton
5. Ellen Miller
6. Kate Holliday
7. Margaret MacDonald
8. Miss Warner
9. Teresa Williams
10. Winifred Gillis

a. Carole Stone
b. Sherry Jackson
c. Florida Friebus
d. Heather Young
e. Elizabeth Fraser
f. Diana Rigg
g. Kathy Coleman
h. Lynda Carter
i. Jan Clayton
j. Rosemary DeCamp

92. AIR WAVES

1. Who played George C. Scott's girlfriend on *East Side/West Side?*

2. At what supper club did Dorothy Provine entertain in *The Roaring Twenties?*

3. Between which two states did the stagecoach line run in *Overland Trail?*

4. The Del Florias Tailor Shop was a front for what international crime-fighting organization?

5. Who was Rootie Kazootie's arch enemy?

6. Name Ben Cartwright's horse.

7. On *Tom Corbett, Space Cadet*, what planets were in the so-called Solar Alliance?

8. Name the newspaper depicted in *Crime Photographer*.

9. At what island was the *P.T. 73* stationed?

10. What was the setting for *Black Saddle?*

93. WHAT...

1. ... was Sugarfoot's name?

2. ... did *SurfSide 6* mean?

3. ... did Jimmy Olsen call Lois Lane?

4. ... famous personality was featured on *Bachelor Haven,* dispensing advice to women about men (a subject she knew well)?

5. ... job did Joanne Jordan have on *This Is Your Life?*

6. ... role did Mary Wickes play on *The Halls of Ivy?*

7. ... was Jay North's name on *Maya?*

8. ... hotel did Byron Glick work at as a house detective?

9. ... program opened with the narration "Democracy is a very bad form of government, but I ask you never to forget it, all the others are so much worse"?

10. ... phone number was the title of a 1961 detective show starring Walter Matthau?

94. JACKIE GLEASON

1. Gleason's loudmouth character Charley Bratton had a favorite victim, played by Art Carney. What was his name?

2. Who portrayed Jackie's son on *The Life of Riley*?

3. With whom did Joe the Bartender often converse?

4. What was Reginald Van Gleason III's father's name?

5. What was Mrs. Manicotti's *(The Honeymooners)* first name?

6. Gleason played a repairman in sketches. What was the not-so-handyman's name?

7. Who was Fenwick Babbitt?

8. Who was Jackie's orchestra leader—Sammy Spear or Ray Bloch?

9. After his brief stint in *The Life of Riley*, Gleason starred in a DuMont network variety show. Name it.

10. Before Joyce Randolph took over the part of Trixie, who played Mrs. Norton?

95. THE MELODY LINGERS ON

Match the theme songs with the programs.

1. "One for My Baby"
2. "Tenderly"
3. "As Long as There's Music"
4. "Whenever I'm with You"
5. "Londonderry Air"
6. "Holiday for Strings"
7. "Thanks for the Memory"
8. "Funeral March of Marionettes"
9. "Mary, I'm in Love With You"
10. "On My Way to a Star"

a. *The Danny Thomas Show*
b. *The Adventures of McGraw*
c. *The Rosemary Clooney Show*
d. *The Red Skelton Show*
e. *The Perry Como Show*
f. *The Bob Hope Show*
g. *Alfred Hitchcock Presents*
h. *The Adventures of Ozzie and Harriet*
i. *The Eddie Fisher Show*
j. *The Paul Winchell Show*

96. LIKELY PAIRS

Identify the actors who portrayed these married couple characters, and name the program.

1. Vicki and Gus Angel
2. Elinor and Walter Hathaway
3. Sylvia and Leo Schnauzer
4. Kay and Roger Addison
5. Louise and Biff Baker
6. Penny and Dick Cooper
7. Joan and Jim Nash
8. Francesca and Joe Girelli
9. Frances and Tom Potter
10. Louise and Larry Tate

97. CHANNELS

1. What was Pete Malloy's badge number?
2. Where does Archie Bunker work?
3. Who is the announcer on *The Match Game?*
4. What is the name of Walter Findlay's business?
5. On what show was the Devil Hole Gang featured?
6. Who conducted *The Bell Telephone Hour* orchestra?
7. Who played Goldie Appleby, a New York manicurist?
8. What famous TV family resided at 518 Crestview Drive in Beverly Hills?
9. Who was the first host of *The Big Payoff?*
10. What was the name of Wednesday Addams's pet spider?

98. TRIPLE THREAT

Identify the actor or actress who appeared as a regular character in each trio of TV series.

1. City Detective/State Trooper/Coronado 9
2. Baileys of Balboa/Fair Exchange/Laugh In
3. The Tammy Grimes Show/Bewitched/Broadside
4. Overland Trail/Search/Barbary Coast
5. The Courtship of Eddie's Father/My Favorite Martian/The Magician
6. Police Woman/Hotel de Paree/Wide Country
7. Batman/The Real McCoys/The Joey Bishop Show
8. The Burns and Allen Show/Petticoat Junction/The Flintstones
9. The Andy Griffith Show/Happy Days/The Smith Family
10. Rhoda/McMillan and Wife/Family Affair

99. GO WEST

Match the western character with the actor who portrayed him.

1. Jim Hardie
2. Flint McCullough
3. Pat Garrett
4. Frank Morgan
5. Vint Bonner
6. Chris Colt
7. Gil Favor
8. Shotgun Slade
9. Johnny Ringo
10. Clay McCord

a. Barry Sullivan
b. Allen Case
c. Don Durant
d. Scott Brady
e. John Payne
f. Eric Fleming
g. Dale Robertson
h. John Bromfield
i. Wayde Preston
j. Robert Horton

ANSWERS

QUIZ 1

1. Turo, Italy
2. Uncle Alberto
3. Johnny Longden
4. Ethel's Uncle Oscar
5. "Glow Worm" or "Sweet Sue"
6. Gale Gordon
7. She disguised it as a baby
8. A Handy Dandy Vacuum Cleaner
9. Betty and Ralph Ramsey
10. Philip Morris cigarettes

QUIZ 2

1. c
2. g
3. e
4. h
5. b
6. k
7. f
8. j
9. d
10. i
11. a

QUIZ 3

1. *Iron Horse*
2. All were hosts of *Death Valley Days*
3. Black Beauty
4. Captain Midnight
5. James Butler Hickok
6. Hopalong Cassidy
7. Arnie
8. Tige
9. Sherman Billingsley
10. Scott Ross and Clipper Hamilton (on *Straightaway*)
11. Renfrew, New Hampshire

QUIZ 4

1. Dick Van Dyke; *The Dick Van Dyke Show* and *The New Dick Van Dyke Show*
2. Andy Griffith; *The Andy Griffith Show* and *The New Andy Griffith Show*
3. Del Moore; *Life With Elizabeth* and *Bachelor Father*
4. Jim Backus; *I Married Joan* and *Gilligan's Island*
5. Dick Sargent; *One Happy Family* and *Bewitched*
6. Leon Ames; *Life With Father* and *Father of the Bride*
7. Larry Keating; *The George Burns and Gracie Allen Show* and *Mr. Ed*
8. Bob Crane; *The Donna Reed Show* and *The Bob Crane Show*
9. John Astin; *I'm Dickens, He's Fenster* and *The Addams Family*
10. Jackie Gleason; *The Life of Riley* and *The Honeymooners*

QUIZ 5

1. *The Tall Man*
2. Chris Jones
3. Laramie, Texas
4. .44-4 Winchester carbine
5. Galen
6. *Have Gun, Will Travel* (starring John Dehner)
7. Buckshot
8. So he would be reminded to use them sparingly
9. Bill Williams
10. Charles Bronson and Ryan O'Neal
11. John Reid

QUIZ 6

1. c
2. i
3. a
4. b
5. e
6. g
7. d
8. j
9. f
10. h

QUIZ 7

1. *All in the Family*
2. *The Andy Griffith Show*
3. *The Danny Thomas Show*
4. *The Mary Tyler Moore Show*
5. *Barney Miller*
6. *Gunsmoke*
7. *Love, American Style*
8. *December Bride*
9. *Petticoat Junction*
10. *Gene Autry*

QUIZ 8

1. Floyd Larsen's
2. Indiana
3. The white knight
4. Bronco's Auto Repairing and Otto's Auto Orphanage
5. Johnson, a one-armed man
6. Wolfie
7. Toy factory
8. The *Calypso*
9. Station 51
10. Sam, the butcher

QUIZ 9

1. Actor and army officer, respectively
2. Franklin Harper, Jeremiah Pike, Bosley Cranston, and Ned Brown
3. Some Artie-created characters
4. Head of Secret Service and Regional Head of Secret Service, respectively
5. Ulysses S. Grant
6. Artie's pigeons
7. Jim and Artie's manservant
8. Train
9. Michael Dunn
10. CBS

QUIZ 10

1. c
2. g
3. h
4. a
5. j
6. b
7. e
8. f
9. d
10. i

QUIZ 11

1. *Space Patrol*
2. Martin Landau
3. *Orbit Jet*
4. Joseph Nash
5. Space Ghost
6. *25th*
7. *The Jetsons*
8. *Planet Patrol*
9. *Jupiter II*
10. Astro Boy

QUIZ 12

1. b
2. f
3. j
4. g
5. a
6. h
7. d
8. e
9. i
10. c

QUIZ 13

1. Asta
2. Pax
3. Duke
4. Gulliver
5. Ivan
6. Paisley
7. Blackjack
8. Neil
9. Lad
10. Lord Nelson

QUIZ 14

1. Leroy and Opalette
2. Dan Laurie
3. Reed Hadley
4. Natasha Fataly
5. Sheila Graham
6. All played the lead in *Foreign Intrigue*
7. Pat Kennedy, series star Peter Lawford's wife
8. Solly, the doctor
9. The Hampstead Apartments as a janitor
10. Crab Apple Cove, Maine

QUIZ 15

1. *The Survivors*
2. *Bachelor Father*
3. *Overland Trail*
4. *Riverboat*
5. *Rawhide*
6. *Wagon Train*
7. *Leave It to Beaver*
8. *Sea Hunt*
9. *The Virginian*
10. *Ironside*

QUIZ 16

1. b
2. g
3. h
4. f
5. a
6. e
7. j
8. i
9. c
10. d

QUIZ 17

1. Tommy Rettig
2. Ellen Miller
3. Sylvester "Porky" Brockway (played by Donald Keeler)
4. Uncle Petrie Martin
5. Cloris Leachman and Jon Shepodd, and then June Lockhart and Hugh Reilly
6. Domino
7. Australia
8. Jenny
9. Ranger Cory Stuart
10. Keith Holden

QUIZ 18

1. Walter Cronkite
2. Edward R. Murrow
3. John Daly
4. Martha Raye
5. John Beresford Tipton (on *The Millionaire*)
6. George Gobel
7. Announcer on *The Beverly Hillbillies*
8. Jimmy Durante
9. Red Skelton
10. Dave Garroway (on *Today*)

QUIZ 19

1. Officer Dibble
2. Frostbite Falls, Minnesota
3. Flagghopple
4. *Super Chicken*
5. Ross Bagdasarian
6. Larry (his mother couldn't spell)
7. Barney found him on his doorstep
8. Dr. Benton Quest
9. Edward Everett Horton
10. Mr. Peebles Pet Shop

QUIZ 20

1. g
2. c
3. h
4. i
5. b
6. j
7. a
8. e
9. f
10. d

QUIZ 21

1. d, Did not play herself on TV
2. b, Bob Denver did not appear on it
3. b, Not featured on *The Virginian*
4. d, Did not play Martin Kane
5. b, Not featured in program set in Hawaii
6. d, Did not feature a character named Mike
7. c, Did not premiere in the fall of 1955
8. d, Only one with two consecutive successful series
9. a, Not hosted by Jack Barry
10. b, Not a June Taylor/*Jackie Gleason Show* dancer

QUIZ 22

1. Chimp J. Fred Muggs's young simian cohort on *Today*
2. Joey was streetfighting when taken into custody. Jim was a witness and assisted in the youngster's defense. The judge allowed Newton to adopt the boy.
3. Edward R. Murrow, Eric Sevareid, and Howard K. Smith
4. Mr. Beasley
5. L.A. *Daily Blade*
6. Mesa Grande
7. One of Jimmy Nelson's puppets
8. At a West Coast broadcasting company as a page
9. All played George Gobel's wife Alice
10. Francis, the stagehand

QUIZ 23

1. Audra Lindley; *Bridget Loves Bernie* and *Three's Company*
2. Emmaline Henry; *I Dream of Jeannie* and *I'm Dickens, He's Fenster*
3. Betty White; *A Date With the Angels* and *Life With Elizabeth*
4. Mabel Albertson; *Bewitched* and *That Girl*
5. Mary Jane Croft; *The Adventures of Ozzie and Harriet* and *I Love Lucy*
6. Lurene Tuttle; *Life With Father* and *Father of the Bride*
7. Pat Carroll; *The Danny Thomas Show* and *Busting Loose*
8. Beverly Garland; *The Bing Crosby Show* and *My Three Sons*
9. Sylvia Field; *Mr. Peepers* and *Dennis the Menace*
10. Cara Williams; *Pete and Gladys* and *The Cara Williams Show*

QUIZ 24

1. Richard Coogan
2. In a mountain peak
3. Don Hastings
4. DuMont
5. 2254 A.D.
6. The *Galaxey*
7. Doctor Tobor
8. Safety of the World
9. Post Cereals
10. It enabled the Captain to spy on anyone anywhere in the world regardless of disguises or solid walls—in other words, an electronic Peeping Tom

QUIZ 25

1. *Gomer Pyle, U.S.M.C.*
2. *Hennessey*
3. *The Rat Patrol*
4. *Twelve O'Clock High*
5. *The Wackiest Ship in the Army*
6. *Combat*
7. *You'll Never Get Rich*
8. *Convoy*
9. *The Gallant Men*
10. *Broadside*

QUIZ 26

1. Freddie, Patty, and Ellen
2. Louise, Mae, and Roberta
3. Charlie, Enoch, and Candy
4. Stoney Burke
5. Ginger Farrell, Ginger Loomis, and Ginger Mitchell
6. Steve, Jr., Charley, and Robbie II
7. Phil Silvers for his portrayal of Sgt. Ernie Bilko
8. *Gidget, The Flying Nun,* and *The Girl With Something Extra*
9. *The Alvin Show*
10. Mary, Jeff, and Trisha

QUIZ 27

1. c
2. a
3. b
4. b
5. a
6. a
7. c
8. b
9. a
10. b

QUIZ 28

1. Oliver J. Dragon III; born at Dragon Retreat, Vermont; attended Dragon Prep
2. Ophelia
3. Colonel Crackie
4. Fletcher Rabbit
5. "Here we are/Back with you again/Yes, by gum, and yes, by golly/Kukla, Fran and dear old Ollie/Here we are again/Here we are again"
6. Burr Tillstrom
7. "Hello, dear!"
8. Cecil Bill
9. Miss Clara Coo Coo
10. She was the spoiled-brat friend of Dolores Dragon, Ollie's niece

QUIZ 29

1. North Cemetery Ridge
2. 160 acres
3. Centerville
4. The *Tonight* show
5. Helen Reddy
6. The town of Diablo
7. Tony Marvin
8. Sally Ann Morrison
9. Bill Baldwin
10. *Believe It or Not*

QUIZ 30

1. Harry Belafonte
2. *Huckleberry Hound*
3. *Faraway Hill* (circa 1946, DuMont network)
4. *Best of Broadway*
5. 1939—Baer versus Nova
6. Groucho Marx
7. Laura Marr Stone, a pioneer woman from Kansas
8. Barton Yarborough as Ben Romero
9. 1939
10. Shirley Dinsdale and her puppet Judy Splinters

QUIZ 31

1. Nelson
2. Basco
3. Weber
4. Armitage
5. Jones
6. Arbuckle
7. Praskins
8. Cooper
9. Blake
10. Whitney

QUIZ 32

1. b
2. e
3. f
4. i
5. c
6. j
7. d
8. g
9. h
10. a

QUIZ 33

1. Los Angeles *Sun*
2. Richard Webb, *Silver Dart*
3. Dolores Rosedale
4. Jason
5. The same host, Bill Leyden
6. John Brewster
7. Sioux
8. Western State University
9. Kathy Jo
10. Bain

QUIZ 34

1. Molly Goldberg
2. El Brendel
3. Bob *(Time for Beany)* Clampett
4. Herburt Vigran
5. Bill Lundigan
6. Jack Benny
7. Mickey Riley
8. Dexter Franklin
9. Bobby Troup
10. Carlo Corelli

QUIZ 35

1. Jack Paar
2. Jack Benny
3. Sue Ane Langdon
4. "Everything's Coming Up Roses"
5. Jack Carson
6. Happy and Walter
7. *Hootenanny*
8. Woofer
9. Jackie Gleason
10. Jackie Joseph

QUIZ 36

1. *Beat the Clock*
2. *Stork Club*
3. *Tom Corbett, Space Cadet*
4. *Strike It Rich*
5. *The Merry Mailman*
6. *You Bet Your Life*
7. *Crime Photographer*
8. *The Aldrich Family*
9. *I Love Lucy*
10. *Amos 'n' Andy*

QUIZ 37

1. *Smilin' Ed's Gang*
2. *This Is Show Business*
3. *Hollywood Screen Test*
4. *Beulah*
5. *Heaven for Betsy*
6. *Those Two*
7. *Juvenile Jury*
8. *Man Against Crime*
9. *Mr. and Mrs. North*
10. *Biff Baker, U.S.A.*

QUIZ 38

1. *The Stu Erwin Show, a/k/a Trouble With Father*
2. *A Date With Judy*
3. *Life Begins at 80*
4. *My Favorite Husband*
5. *Rod Brown of the Rocket Rangers*
6. *The Dave Garroway Show*
7. *My Son Jeep*
8. *Atom Squad*
9. *Place the Face*
10. *Mama*

QUIZ 39

1. Topper
2. The Paul Hartman Show, a/k/a Pride of the Family
3. Cowboy G-Men
4. Sky King
5. Mr. Peepers
6. I Led Three Lives
7. Breakfast Club
8. Winky Dink and You
9. The Ray Bolger Show, a/k/a Where's Raymond?
10. The Big Payoff

QUIZ 40

1. Mr. Wizard
2. Professional Father
3. It's a Great Life
4. The Line-Up
5. Youth Wants to Know
6. You Asked for It
7. Howdy Doody
8. Meet Millie
9. The Bob Cummings Show
10. Waterfront

QUIZ 41

1. *Annie Oakley*
2. *Soldiers of Fortune*
3. *My Hero*
4. *I Search for Adventure*
5. *Lassie*
6. *The Charlie Farrell Show*
7. *Zane Grey Theatre*
8. *My Friend Flicka*
9. *The Crusader*
10. *Noah's Ark*

QUIZ 42

1. *Big Top*
2. *December Bride*
3. *Wire Service*
4. *Those Whiting Girls*
5. *Broken Arrow*
6. *The Eve Arden Show*
7. *Mr. Adams and Eve*
8. *The Thin Man*
9. *Judge Roy Bean*
10. *Dick and the Duchess*

QUIZ 43

1. *The Adventures of Rin Tin Tin*
2. *Tugboat Annie*
3. *The Real McCoys*
4. *Bachelor Father*
5. *Sea Hunt*
6. *City Detective*
7. *Code 3*
8. *Trackdown*
9. *Wells Fargo*
10. *M Squad*

QUIZ 44

1. *77 Sunset Strip*
2. *Rawhide*
3. *21 Beacon Street*
4. *The Deputy*
5. *Buckskin*
6. *Wanted—Dead or Alive*
7. *Riverboat*
8. *The Rebel*
9. *Hennessey*
10. *Men Into Space*

QUIZ 45

1. *Route 66*
2. *Coronado 9*
3. *The Danny Thomas Show*
4. *How to Marry a Millionaire*
5. *The Tom Ewell Show*
6. *The Ann Sothern Show*
7. *Guestward Ho!*
8. *Hey, Jeannie*
9. *My Three Sons*
10. *Bringing Up Buddy*

QUIZ 46

1. *Father of the Bride*
2. *The Flintstones*
3. *Ripcord*
4. *The Dick Van Dyke Show*
5. *Checkmate*
6. *King of Diamonds*
7. *Ichabod and Me*
8. *The Beachcomber*
9. *Car 54, Where Are You?*
10. *Ben Casey*

QUIZ 47

1. *Fair Exchange*
2. *The Adventures of Ozzie and Harriet*
3. *The Donna Reed Show*
4. *The Aquanauts*
5. *Empire*
6. *The Third Man*
7. *Going My Way*
8. *It's a Man's World*
9. *McKeever and the Colonel*
10. *Gunsmoke*

QUIZ 48

1. *Petticoat Junction*
2. *Harry's Girls*
3. *The Travels of Jaimie McPheeters*
4. *The Farmer's Daughter*
5. *East Side/West Side*
6. *The Many Loves of Dobie Gillis*
7. *The New Phil Silvers Show*
8. *The Lieutenant*
9. *The Patty Duke Show*
10. *The Bill Dana Show*

QUIZ 49

1. *The Reporter*
2. *The Man From U.N.C.L.E.*
3. *McHale's Navy*
4. *Peyton Place*
5. *The Baileys of Balboa*
6. *The Tycoon*
7. *That Was the Week That Was*
8. *Shindig*
9. *Many Happy Returns*
10. *No Time for Sergeants*

QUIZ 50

1. *The Smothers Brothers Show*
2. *Convoy*
3. *Hank*
4. *Camp Runamuck*
5. *The Long, Hot Summer*
6. *I Spy*
7. *Lost in Space*
8. *F Troop*
9. *Please Don't Eat the Daisies*
10. *Combat*

QUIZ 51

1. *Time Tunnel*
2. *Tarzan*
3. *That Girl*
4. *Family Affair*
5. *Jericho*
6. *Green Acres*
7. *Love on a Rooftop*
8. *The Rounders*
9. *Run for Your Life*
10. *Rat Patrol*

QUIZ 52

1. *Accidental Family*
2. *Bewitched*
3. *Good Company*
4. *He and She*
5. *Secret Agent*
6. *N.Y.P.D.*
7. *Daktari*
8. *Twelve O'Clock High*
9. *Maya*
10. *The Second Hundred Years*

QUIZ 53

1. *The Guns of Will Sonnett*
2. *Gentle Ben*
3. *The Outsider*
4. *Julia*
5. *The Don Rickles Show*
6. *The Flying Nun*
7. *The Good Guys*
8. *It Takes a Thief*
9. *The Mothers-In-Law*
10. *That's Life*

QUIZ 54

1. *Bracken's World*
2. *The Name of the Game*
3. *Daniel Boone*
4. *The Ghost and Mrs. Muir*
5. *Mayberry, R.F.D.*
6. *The Bill Cosby Show*
7. *Lassie*
8. *The High Chaparral*
9. *Adam-12*
10. *Room 222*

QUIZ 55

1. *The Brady Bunch*
2. *The Interns*
3. *Nancy*
4. *Medical Center*
5. *The Courtship of Eddie's Father*
6. *The Young Lawyers*
7. *Wild Kingdom*
8. *Headmaster*
9. *The Mod Squad*
10. *Barefoot in the Park*

QUIZ 56

1. *Bearcat!*
2. *Alias Smith and Jones*
3. *Sarge*
4. *The Smith Family*
5. *The Partners*
6. *Shirley's World*
7. *The Partridge Family*
8. *The Funny Side*
9. *Arnie*
10. *Cade's County*

QUIZ 57

1. *Assignment: Vienna*
2. *Search*
3. *Temperature's Rising*
4. *Bridget Loves Bernie*
5. *The Little People*
6. *Ironside*
7. *The Delphi Bureau*
8. *The Waltons*
9. *Cool Million*
10. *The Paul Lynde Show*

QUIZ 58

1. *Adam's Rib*
2. *Needles and Pins*
3. *The Girl With Something Extra*
4. *Calucci's Department*
5. *Maude*
6. *Lotsa Luck!*
7. *Kung Fu*
8. *The Magician*
9. *The Streets of San Francisco*
10. *Roll Out!*

QUIZ 59

1. *Movin' On*
2. *Paper Moon*
3. *Good Times*
4. *That's My Mama*
5. *Born Free*
6. *The Rookies*
7. *Upstairs, Downstairs*
8. *The Rockford Files*
9. *The Texas Wheelers*
10. *Sons and Daughters*

QUIZ 60

1. *Big Eddie*
2. *The Bob Newhart Show*
3. *The Montefuscos*
4. *Barney Miller*
5. *Rhoda*
6. *Police Woman*
7. *Joe and Sons*
8. *Welcome Back, Kotter*
9. *Happy Days*
10. *One Day at a Time*

QUIZ 61

1. *Mary Hartman, Mary Hartman*
2. *Spencer's Pilots*
3. *The Tony Randall Show*
4. *Gemini Man*
5. *The Bionic Woman*
6. *The Quest*
7. *Ball Four*
8. *Switch*
9. *All's Fair*
10. *The Jeffersons*

QUIZ 62

1. *Carter Country*
2. *Busting Loose*
3. *Sirota's Court*
4. *Man From Atlantis*
5. *We've Got Each Other*
6. *Operation Petticoat*
7. *Oregon Trail*
8. *Grizzly Adams*
9. *Alice*
10. *The Betty White Show*

QUIZ 63

1. c
2. f
3. j
4. d
5. i
6. e
7. h
8. g
9. a
10. b

QUIZ 64

1. Fury
2. Catherine
3. July 2, 1842
4. Tumbly, Iowa
5. "Puce Goose" and "Blond Blintz," respectively
6. Sarah and David
7. Chester's niece from Brooklyn (played by Lorraine Bendix, William Bendix's real-life daughter)
8. Millie Hutchins
9. Charger
10. Lala

QUIZ 65

1. c
2. f
3. j
4. e
5. i
6. a
7. h
8. g
9. b
10. d

QUIZ 66

1. First at the all-girl Newton University as an English professor; then at Comstock University as drama professor
2. Oxford University
3. Cooking
4. Stretch Snodgrass
5. Burgess Meredith
6. Seymour
7. Helen Watkins
8. Beaver Cleaver's
9. Anthropology
10. Hamilton High School

QUIZ 67

1. Barbara Boylan
2. "Ta-Ra-Ra Boom-der-e"
3. Dr. Bombay
4. The Treasure House
5. Kelly
6. *Sheena, Queen of the Jungle*
7. Connie Brooks as a drama teacher
8. Frederic
9. *The Mask*
10. Maurice Marsac

QUIZ 68

1. Perry Como
2. *Your Show of Shows*
3. Garry Moore
4. Danny Kaye
5. Jerry Lewis
6. *The Smothers Brothers Comedy Hour*
7. *The New Bill Cosby Show*
8. *Saturday Night Revue*
9. *The Milton Berle Show*
10. Red Skelton

QUIZ 69

1. Roy
2. Candy
3. Warren
4. Sardius
5. Phil
6. Will
7. Cicero P.
8. Herb
9. Louis
10. Jerome

QUIZ 70

1. Clarabell Hornblow Clown
2. False; he spoke once on the last show, saying, "Goodbye, kids." Lew Anderson, who played him then, said it
3. Seventy-two
4. "America's Number One [BOING!] Private Eye"
5. Air-O-Doodle
6. Welch's, Wonder Bread, Burry Cookies, Royal Jell-O, Mars Candy, Hostess Twinkies, Ovaltine, Tootsie Rolls, Poll-Parrott Shoes, Colgate-Palmolive, and Unique Art Toys
7. He had two horns: a "yes" and a "no"
8. Captain Windy Scuttlebutt
9. J. Cornelius Cobb
10. Judy Tyler

QUIZ 71

1. Two of Mr. Wizard's mid-fifties "students," Buzz and Betty
2. Pincus Pines
3. 22 Wood Avenue, Metropolis
4. The First National Bank on Main Street, as vice president in charge of small loans
5. Edward R. Murrow
6. Bergen Evans
7. Tennessee Ernie Ford
8. *U.S. Steel Hour* (1955)
9. *Sherlock Holmes*
10. Rochelle Hudson

QUIZ 72

1. b
2. a
3. i
4. h
5. f
6. j
7. g
8. c
9. d
10. e

QUIZ 73

1. b
2. j
3. g
4. i
5. a
6. h
7. e
8. d
9. f
10. c

QUIZ 74

1. f
2. b
3. g
4. i
5. j
6. e
7. a
8. d
9. h
10. c

QUIZ 75

1. "Do you recall, or remember at all, that wonderful, wonderful year?"
2. "So long for a while/That's all the songs for a while/So long to *Your Hit Parade*/And the tunes that you picked to be played/So long"
3. Ray Ellis
4. Johnny Cash
5. *The Ernie Kovacs Show*
6. *Captain Nice*
7. The Roger Wagner Chorale
8. "You Are So Rare to Me"
9. Yancy Derringer
10. The Ken Darby Singers

QUIZ 76

1. David Wayne
2. Cesar Romero
3. Frank Gorshin and John Astin
4. Burgess Meredith
5. Victor Buono
6. Julie Newmar, Lee Meriweather, and Eartha Kitt
7. Otto Preminger and George Sanders
8. Art Carney
9. Vincent Price
10. Shelley Winters

QUIZ 77

1. Navy Day, 1945
2. *Mr. Smith Goes to Washington*
3. "Solfeggio," based on a theme by Bach
4. Code words for London and the Stalag 13 captives, respectively
5. January 4, 1971
6. L.A. "Speed" Riggs of Reidsville, North Carolina
7. Ronzoni
8. Indian attack
9. Frump
10. T.R. Ryan, Mama's nephew

QUIZ 78

1. g and t
2. b and r
3. n and s
4. f and q
5. h and p
6. a and m
7. e and o
8. d and i
9. j and l
10. c and k

QUIZ 79

1. *Search for Tomorrow*
2. *Love of Life*
3. *Hawkins Falls*
4. *The Guiding Light*
5. *Brighter Day*
6. *Valiant Lady*
7. *Three Steps to Heaven*
8. *The Inner Flame*
9. *Miss Marlowe*
10. *Seeking Heart*

QUIZ 80

1. Twirl
2. Pepto-Bismol
3. Westinghouse
4. Winston
5. Gleem
6. Chesterfield
7. Bufferin
8. Chevrolet
9. Alka-Seltzer
10. Rin-So White

QUIZ 81

1. b, *The Thin Man*
2. e, *People Are Funny*
3. d, *Father Knows Best*
4. c, *Martin Kane*
5. j, *Meet Corliss Archer*
6. h, *Red Ryder*
7. a, *Queen for a Day*
8. g, *Nick Carter*
9. i, *Ellery Queen*
10. f, *Mr. District Attorney*

QUIZ 82

1. Thompson
2. Allan "Rocky" Lane
3. Aloysius
4. El Toro
5. 3
6. Volvo P-1800
7. *Stagecoach West*
8. *My Three Sons* (twelve years)
9. Ernie Kovacs'
10. Jackson Beck

QUIZ 83

1. 932
2. Bill
3. 12
4. Hempel's Department Store
5. Dermatologist
6. Dotty and Walter Richards
7. Marie and Edie, respectively
8. Franklin
9. Sonny Curtis
10. Larry Gelman

QUIZ 84

1. Polly
2. LaVerne
3. Agnes
4. Barbara
5. Helen
6. Catherine
7. Martha
8. Jenny
9. Helen
10. Joanne

QUIZ 85

1. b
2. c
3. j
4. a
5. i
6. e
7. g
8. f
9. h
10. d

QUIZ 86

1. Paul Fonda (played by Lyle Talbot)
2. 732
3. Merdle
4. Bronson
5. Danny Williams
6. Ann Baker
7. Bert Convy
8. Walter (named after his aunt)
9. Bronx, Harlem, child, Idlewyld
10. 378 years old

QUIZ 87

1. 744
2. 101st Cavalry
3. 054-22-5457
4. 402
5. Forty-four
6. 60611
7. 416
8. C12 563
9. 10610918
10. 318th

QUIZ 88

1. Ben
2. Ed
3. Louie
4. Jack
5. Kevin
6. Julius Caesar
7. Harry
8. Chris
9. Harry
10. Jim

QUIZ 89

1. Psychology as a teacher
2. Sixth grade
3. Smiff
4. Toastettes
5. Their hostess, Arlene Francis
6. *One Minute, Please*
7. *The Morning Show*
8. Nancy Walker
9. Miss Frances on *Ding Dong School*
10. A windbag character played by Red Buttons

QUIZ 90

1. *Amos 'n' Andy*
2. *The Andy Griffith Show*
3. *The Life of Riley*
4. *The Honeymooners*
5. *The Real McCoys*
6. *The Flintstones*
7. *All in the Family*
8. *The Charlie Farrell Show*
9. *I Love Lucy*
10. *Mama*

QUIZ 91

1. f
2. h
3. g
4. d
5. i
6. a
7. j
8. e
9. b
10. c

QUIZ 92

1. Barbara Feldon
2. The Charleston Club
3. California and Missouri
4. United Network Command for Law Enforcement (U.N.C.L.E.)
5. Poison Sumac
6. Buck
7. Earth, Mars, Venus, and Jupiter
8. *Morning Express*
9. Taratoopa
10. Marathon Hotel in Latigo, New Mexico

QUIZ 93

1. Tom Brewster
2. It was the address of the houseboat
3. Miss Lane
4. Zsa Zsa Gabor
5. She was the commercial spokeswoman for Hazel Bishop Cosmetics who used to paint her palm with lipstick
6. Alice, the maid
7. Terry Bowen
8. The Metropolitan Hotel
9. *Slattery's People*
10. Tallahassee 7000

QUIZ 94

1. Clem Finch
2. Lanny Rees
3. Crazy Guggenheim and, off camera, Mr. Dennchy
4. Sedgwick Van Gleason, played by Art Carney
5. Angelina
6. Rudy
7. A harassed clerk whom Gleason played
8. Both
9. *Cavalcade of Stars*
10. Elaine Stritch

QUIZ 95

1. b
2. c
3. i
4. j
5. a
6. d
7. f
8. g
9. h
10. e

QUIZ 96

1. Betty White and Bill Williams, *A Date With the Angels*
2. Peggy Cass and Jack Weston, *The Hathaways*
3. Charlotte Rae and Al Lewis, *Car 54, Where Are You?*
4. Edna Skinner and Larry Keating, *Mr. Ed*
5. Randy Stuart and Alan Hale, Jr., *Biff Baker, U.S.A.*
6. Jodie Warner and Dick Sargent, *One Happy Family*
7. Patricia Crowley and Mark Miller, *Please Don't Eat the Daisies*
8. Ardell Sheridan and Richard Castellano, *The Super*
9. Marilyn Erskine and Tom Ewell, *The Tom Ewell Show*
10. Irene Vernon and David White, *Bewitched*

QUIZ 97

1. 2430
2. At the Pendergast Tool and Die Company as a dock foreman
3. Johnny Olsen
4. Findlay's Friendly Appliances
5. *Alias Smith and Jones*
6. Donald Voorhees
7. Betty Hutton
8. *The Beverly Hillbillies*
9. Bert Parks
10. Homer

QUIZ 98

1. Rod Cameron
2. Judy Carne
3. Dick Sargent
4. Doug McClure
5. Bill Bixby
6. Earl Holliman
7. Madge Blake
8. Bea Benaderet
9. Ron Howard
10. Nancy Walker

QUIZ 99

1. g
2. j
3. a
4. h
5. e
6. i
7. f
8. d
9. c
10. b

PHOTO ANALYSIS

1. Botany
2. The Garrytone News
3. 607 South Maple Street, Springfield
4. The Carlton Arms, New York City
5. LU 2-3100
6. Jack Paar, Genevieve
7. Gerald Lloyd Kookson, III
8. Sylvester L. "Pat" Weaver